THE BARNDOMINIUM BUILDER'S HANDBOOK

From Blueprint to Homefront, Planning to Permits, and Pallets to Paint

Expert Advice for Every Step of Your Home-Building Adventure

HARPER BENTON

Contents

Introduction

Who would've thought that marrying a barn with a condominium could create such a stir in the housing market? Well, welcome to the world of barndominiums, where rustic meets modern and where your dream home doesn't have to break the bank. If you're looking for a sign to ditch the cookie-cutter houses for something uniquely yours, this might just be it.

Hey there, I'm your guide on this exciting adventure of transforming beams and barn doors into cozy living spaces that scream "you." I'm not just a fan of barndominiums; I'm a full-blown advocate for turning these versatile structures into dream homes. With a hammer of passion and nails of determination, I've spent years helping folks like you navigate the maze of building or converting their very own barndominium. And now, I've poured all that experience, all those insights, and a couple of laughs into this book to offer you the most straightforward, friendly advice on making your barndominium dream a reality.

This book is your all-access pass to the ins and outs of barndominium living. From getting those initial ideas off the ground (literally) to putting the final touches on your dream space, I've got you covered. I'll walk you through the often-daunting permitting process, help you sidestep common pitfalls, and even show you how to keep your wallet from running away screaming. I've been there, done that, and now I'm handing the blueprint of success over to you.

With a background steeped in the dust and triumphs of barndominium construction, I bring to the table a wealth of practical, real-world knowledge. This isn't just theory; it's the nitty-gritty, the successes, the "oops" moments, and everything in between. Whether you're converting an old barn into a snug abode or starting from scratch, this guide has got you covered.

What sets this book apart? It's more than just a collection of tips and tricks. It's a roadmap to saving money, understanding complex permitting systems, and actual step-by-step plans that take you from dreamer to dweller. I'm talking to you, the DIY enthusiasts, the eco-conscious builders, and everyone who's ever thought, "Hey, I want something different for my living space. Wouldn't it be great if …"

So, if you're ready to roll up your sleeves and dive into the world of barndominiums, let's turn those dreams into tangible, livable, and loveable homes. Consider this book your trusty companion on a journey of discovery and empowerment. Together, we'll build not just a house but your home, brimming with personality, efficiency, and, most importantly, a reflection of you. Let's get started, shall we?

ONE

The Evolution of Barndominiums: From Barns to Homes

In the lush landscapes of rural living, where the horizon stretches endlessly and the sky meets the earth, a transformation quietly unfolds—a fusion of tradition and innovation, simplicity and sophistication. This change is not just about architecture or design; it's about reimagining the essence of home. It's about barndominiums.

Once, the barn was a symbol of agricultural life, a place for storing hay or sheltering livestock. Today, it represents something more, something profound—a canvas for personal expression and sustainable living. This shift from the utilitarian to the imaginative embodies the evolution of barndominiums. It's a story that unfolds in the hearts of those seeking a different kind of dwelling—one that pays homage to the past while boldly stepping into the future.

Transformation and Innovation: The Metamorphosis of Barndominiums

Initially, barns were purely functional, serving the needs of farmers for storage and shelter. However, as urban sprawl increased and rural landscapes changed, these structures began to lose their original purpose. It was then that a vision emerged—a vision to repurpose these sturdy, spacious buildings into something more than just agricultural staples.

The term "barndominium" itself is a testament to this transformation. It reflects a unique blend of barn architecture and condominium comfort, embodying the fusion of rustic charm with modern living spaces. This metamorphosis from barns to barndominiums wasn't just about changing the function of a structure; it was about redefining the concept of home for countless individuals and families.

The growing popularity of barndominiums can be attributed to several factors, but none more compelling than their versatility and cost-effectiveness. In an age where housing prices soar, and homeowners seek more bang for their buck, barndominiums offer a compelling alternative. They provide ample space, durability, and the opportunity for customization at a fraction of the cost of traditional homes. Their appeal is broad, attracting not just those looking to live in rural areas but also individuals in suburban and urban settings who yearn for a slice of country living without leaving the conveniences of modern life behind.

Design flexibility is another hallmark of the barndominium evolution. Unlike conventional homes, which often come with predefined layouts and limitations, barndominiums are a blank slate. They invite homeowners to dream big, to design living spaces that truly reflect their needs, tastes, and personalities. From open-concept living areas that foster family togetherness to cozy nooks that offer solitude and reflection, the possibilities are as boundless as one's imagination.

Amid this evolution, sustainability and efficiency have become central themes. Barndominiums, with their spacious interiors and durable materials, are ideally suited for incorporating green building practices. Features like solar panels, rainwater harvesting systems, and energy-efficient windows are not just add-ons; they're integral to the design, reflecting a growing awareness of our environmental footprint and a commitment to reducing it. This shift toward sustainability is not merely a trend but a reflection of a deeper understanding of our relationship with the environment and our responsibility toward it.

The transformation of barns into barndominiums is more than just a change in architecture; it's a movement toward redefining what it means to create a home. It's about building spaces that are not only beautiful and practical but also reflective of the values and aspirations of those who dwell within them. In this evolution, every beam, every wall, and every window tells a story—a story of innovation, of tradition reimagined, and of a future built on the foundation of the past.

Defining Your Barndominium Dreams: Aligning Expectations With Reality

Crafting the vision for your barndominium is an exhilarating process, filled with dreams of expansive living areas, rustic charm, and modern amenities. Yet, this initial excitement must be tempered with a dose of reality. The bridge between what you envision and what's achievable often rests on several key pillars: understanding your true needs, budgeting wisely, planning for the future, and anticipating challenges.

Vision Setting

Imagine waking up each morning in a space that feels authentically yours. This is the heart of the barndominium appeal. To get there, start by picturing your ideal lifestyle. Do you yearn for vast, open spaces where your family can gather or cozy corners for solitude and creativity? Think about the elements that draw you to the barndominium concept. Is it the blend of traditional and contemporary, the allure of a simpler life, or the flexibility to craft a home that breaks the mold of conventional living? Your vision for your barndominium should mirror the life you wish to lead, blending aesthetic desires with practical needs. Consider everything from the number of bedrooms to the flow between living, working, and outdoor spaces.

Budget Considerations

Next, let's talk numbers. Dream homes only become a reality through thoughtful and realistic budgeting. Start by setting a clear budget that accounts for land, construction, design, furnishings, and unforeseen costs. It's crucial to maintain a balance between what you want and what you can afford without stretching yourself too thin. Research the average costs of building a barndominium in your area, and don't forget to factor in expenses like permits, utilities, and interior finishes. One effective strategy is to categorize your budget into "must-haves," "nice-to-haves," and "if-the-budget-allows," ensuring you cover essentials before indulging in extras. Remember, the goal is to build a home that brings joy without financial strain.

Long-Term Planning

A home is more than a place to sleep; it's a space that evolves with you. When dreaming up your barndominium, it's wise to think ahead. Consider how your needs might change over time. Are you planning a family, or will you need to accommodate aging parents? Perhaps a home office or a workshop is on your wish list. Designing with adaptability in mind ensures your barndominium remains a perfect fit for years to come. For example, choosing a layout that allows for easy modifications or additions can save you significant hassle and expense in the future. Also, investing in quality materials and sustainable features can enhance your home's longevity and resale value.

Challenges and Solutions

No matter how well-planned, every construction project encounters its share of hurdles. The key is to anticipate these challenges and arm yourself with solutions. One common obstacle is navigating the permitting process, which can be complex and vary greatly by location. Start by researching local building codes and zoning laws early, and consider hiring a professional to help streamline this process. Another challenge is managing the construction timeline and budget. Delays can be costly and frustrating. To mitigate this, choose experienced contractors with proven track records and establish clear communication from the start. Be sure to include a contingency fund in your budget for unexpected expenses, typically 10–20% of the overall budget, to cover surprises without derailing your project.

In essence, building a barndominium is an exercise in balancing dreams with reality. It requires a clear vision, careful budgeting, thoughtful long-term planning, and a proactive approach to challenges. By keeping these factors in mind, you can navigate the path from dream to reality with confidence and clarity, creating a home that not only meets your needs but also exceeds your expectations.

The Appeal of the Barndominium Lifestyle: Sustainability Meets Design

Living in a barndominium is much like having a canvas where every stroke of the brush reflects a commitment to blending sustainability with personalized design. This unique lifestyle offers a multitude of benefits, from economic savings to a deep connection with the surrounding environment, all while providing a space that uniquely mirrors the dweller's personality and values.

Cost-Effectiveness

Barndominiums stand out as a model of economic and environmental cost-effectiveness. Initially, the savings begin with the construction process. Utilizing a pre-existing barn structure or opting for a barndominium kit can significantly reduce the financial burden compared to traditional home building. The use of metal in many barndominium designs, for example, offers durability and resistance against pests and weather, translating into lower maintenance and insurance costs over time. Furthermore, the energy-saving potential of barndominiums, through the incorporation of eco-friendly materials and technologies, can substantially lower utility bills. This dual aspect of cost-effectiveness not only benefits homeowners financially but also contributes to a smaller environmental footprint.

Eco-Friendly Living

The inherent design of barndominiums lends itself well to sustainable living. Large, open spaces allow for efficient heating and cooling, reducing energy consumption. Many barndominium owners take this a step further by incorporating renewable energy sources, such as solar panels, to power their homes. Rainwater harvesting systems can also be integrated, providing an eco-friendly water source for landscaping and agricultural needs. The choice of materials plays a crucial role, with many opting for recycled, locally sourced, or sustainable options that reduce the environmental impact of construction. This commitment to eco-friendly living not only aligns with a growing societal push toward sustainability but also offers a practical, everyday application of these principles.

Community and Lifestyle

Choosing a barndominium is as much about embracing a certain lifestyle as it is about the home itself. Many find that this lifestyle fosters a stronger connection to nature, with expansive windows and outdoor living spaces that blur the lines between indoor and outdoor living. This connection extends to a sense of community that is often fostered among barndominium dwellers, whether through shared interests in sustainability, agriculture, or simply a love for the unique. For many, the barndominium lifestyle is synonymous with slowing down, enjoying the simpler moments, and fostering relationships with neighbors and the natural world.

Custom Design Benefits

One of the most appealing aspects of the barndominium lifestyle is the ability to design a space that perfectly suits one's personal and environmental needs. Unlike traditional homes, which often come with limited floor plans and customization options, barndominiums are a blank slate. Owners have the freedom to design open, multifunctional spaces that reflect their lifestyle, from incorporating large workshop areas to designing an entire wall of windows to capture passive solar heat and scenic views. This level of customization not only ensures that the home fits the owner's needs like a glove but also allows for the integration of sustainable design elements from the ground up. For those passionate about reducing their environmental impact, this means the opportunity to design a home that leverages natural lighting, minimizes energy use, and uses materials in a way that aligns with eco-friendly principles.

Living in a barndominium represents a choice to prioritize sustainability, cost-effectiveness, and a deep personal connection to one's living space. It's about creating a home that not only shelters but also reflects a commitment to a lifestyle that values the environment, community, and individual expression. In a world where homes are often seen as mere structures, barndominiums stand out as a testament to what happens when design meets purpose, offering a blueprint for living that is both sustainable and deeply satisfying.

Cost-Effective Living in a Custom Home: The Financial Benefits Of Barndominiums

When it comes to choosing a home, the heart often wants what the wallet fears. However, barndominiums stand out as a beacon of hope, balancing aspiration with affordability. This delicate dance between desire and dollars is where barndominiums truly shine, offering a way to craft your dream home without the financial nightmare.

Upfront Costs vs. Long-Term Savings

The initial price tag of constructing a barndominium might raise eyebrows, but it's the long game that we're playing here. For starters, the cost of erecting a barndominium can be significantly lower than that of traditional homes, especially if you're converting an existing barn. But the real magic happens over time. Think about it: energy-efficient designs, durable materials, and lower property taxes in rural locales all contribute to a wallet-friendly living situation over the years. It's like opting for a hybrid car; you pay a bit more upfront for the technology, but the savings at the gas pump make it worth your while.

Material Choices

Selecting materials for your barndominium isn't just about picking what looks good; it's about finding the sweet spot between cost, durability, and sustainability. Metal, often used in barndominium construction, boasts longevity and minimal maintenance, translating into savings down the line. On the insulation front, spray foam might cost a bit more initially but can slash heating and cooling bills by a significant margin. Even the choice between traditional wood and composite materials for decks or accents can affect both your upfront costs and the long-term sustainability of your home. It's about making informed choices that align with both your budget and your values.

DIY Possibilities

Rolling up your sleeves and diving into some DIY projects can not only trim costs but also infuse your home with a sense of personal accomplishment. From interior finishes to constructing outbuildings, the DIY route empowers homeowners to cut labor costs and customize to their heart's content. Imagine laying your own flooring, tile by tile, or painting walls with colors that speak to your soul. This hands-on approach isn't just cost-effective; it's deeply satisfying. Of course, it's crucial to know your limits—some tasks are best left to the pros, but there's a wide range of work that's perfectly suited for the ambitious homeowner.

Resale Value Considerations

While the concept of home is often rooted in permanence, life's unpredictability means resale value should never be ignored. Barndominiums, with their unique blend of charm and functionality, can stand out in the housing market. Their energy efficiency, modern amenities, and distinctive character can make them appealing to a broad audience. However, customization comes with a caveat: overly personal touches might not resonate with all buyers. Striking a balance between customization for your enjoyment and maintaining broad appeal can help ensure your barndominium holds its value. Think timeless, not trendy, and you'll set the stage for a home that's not just a joy to live in but also a wise investment.

In the realm of barndominiums, the fusion of cost-effectiveness and customization creates a living environment that's as financially savvy as it is soulful. The journey from blueprint to reality is paved with decisions that balance the dreams of today with the needs of tomorrow, crafting spaces that are not just houses but homes that resonate with the rhythm of rural life.

Navigating the World of Barndominiums: A Beginner's Guide

Diving into the barndominium lifestyle starts with a solid grasp of the basics—what these unique homes are all about, their standout features, and the perks they bring to the table. A barndominium blends the rustic charm of a barn with the modern comforts and efficiency of a condominium. These structures stand out for their spacious, open floor plans, durable construction materials, and incredible potential for customization. They're as suited to serene country living as they are to bustling family life, offering a canvas for sustainable living practices and personal expression.

Understanding the Basics

At its core, a barndominium is about reimagining traditional spaces for contemporary living. Picture vast, airy interiors with high ceilings, large windows that welcome natural light, and floors that extend as far as the eye can see. The adaptability of these spaces allows for an array of design choices, from loft bedrooms to expansive workshops. This architectural freedom is paired with a practical side—energy efficiency, durability, and reduced maintenance needs—thanks to the use of materials like steel and concrete. The essence of barndominium living is creating a home that's as unique as its inhabitants, all while embracing a lifestyle that values simplicity, sustainability, and personal flair.

Starting the Journey

For those new to the concept, the path to realizing a barndominium dream begins with a few critical steps:

- **Financing**: It is imperative to start gaining financing as early as possible; many financial institutions are still leery of barndominiums, so some patience and creativity may be necessary.

- **Land Purchase**: Securing the right parcel of land is your first step. Look for a spot that resonates with your vision of home, keeping in mind factors like local climate, soil stability, access to utilities, and proximity to amenities. It's not just about the view—consider potential challenges like zoning restrictions or environmental protections that could impact your build.

- **Design Planning**: Once you have your land, it's time to sketch out your vision. Full consideration needs to be given to the positioning of your home. Which direction will it face? Where will the main entry be in relation to the property's driveway? Is there a view to be made the most of? Start with a broad overview of your needs and desires —how many rooms, the importance of natural light, indoor-outdoor flow, etc. At this stage, having a design style in mind—modern, rustic, industrial, or perhaps contemporary—is great for steering you along, but keeping an open mind and gathering as many ideas as possible is crucial.

- **Budget Setting**: With a rough design in hand, begin outlining a budget. Factor in not just construction costs but also land preparation, permits, interior finishes, and a buffer for unexpected expenses. This financial blueprint will guide your project and help avoid overextension.

- **Permitting Process**: Get familiar with local building codes and permit requirements. This bureaucratic step can be time-consuming, but it is essential for legal and safety reasons. Understanding what's needed early on can save headaches down the line.

- **Insurance**: As with all mortgages, the topic of homeowners insurance is always a pain point, but possibly more so with a barndominium. Yep, you've guessed it; insurance companies are also leery of barndos. However, the good news is that once found, the insurance should be less expensive due to the safety and sturdiness of the structure.

Resource Gathering

Building a barndominium is a multifaceted process that benefits greatly from a wealth of information and inspiration. Here are some resources to tap into:

- **Books and Magazines**: There's a growing library of literature dedicated to barndominiums, covering everything from design ideas to technical building guides. These can be invaluable for both inspiration and practical advice.
- **Websites and Blogs**: The internet is awash in resources, from builders' portfolios showcasing past projects to blogs chronicling personal barndominium journeys. Sites like Pinterest can also be gold mines for design and décor ideas.
- **Community Forums**: Online communities, such as Reddit or specialized forums, offer a platform to connect with others who are at various stages of their barndominium projects. Here, you can ask questions, share experiences, and get feedback from a supportive community.
- **Social Media**: Platforms like Instagram or YouTube are fantastic for visual inspiration and learning. Follow hashtags or channels dedicated to barndominiums to see a wide range of designs and learn from others' experiences.

Professional Consultation

While the DIY spirit runs strong in the barndominium community, consulting with professionals can elevate your project from good to great. Architects and builders experienced in barndominium projects can offer insights you might not have considered, from optimizing your layout for energy efficiency to navigating the complexities of local building codes. They can also help with the following:

- **Translate Vision into Reality**: Professionals can take your ideas and craft them into a feasible, detailed plan, ensuring your vision is both architecturally sound and aligned with your budget.
- **Mitigate Challenges**: Experienced pros are adept at foreseeing potential issues, whether it's with land, design, or construction. Their expertise can help sidestep problems that might derail your project or inflate costs.
- **Ensure Quality**: A skilled builder can ensure that your barndominium is constructed to the highest standards, using the right materials and techniques for durability, efficiency, and beauty.
- **Save Time and Money**: While it might seem counterintuitive, investing in expert advice can actually save money in the long run by avoiding costly mistakes and ensuring the project stays on track.

Navigating the initial stages of building a barndominium requires a blend of creativity, practicality, and diligence. By understanding the basics, carefully planning your journey, gathering a wealth of resources, and seeking professional guidance, you can lay a strong foundation for creating a home that's not just a place to live but a reflection of your dreams and values.

TWO

Planning Your Barndominium Budget like a Pro

Imagine piecing together a jigsaw puzzle where each piece represents a different cost associated with building your dream barndominium. Some pieces are larger, like the land and construction costs, while others are smaller yet crucial, like permits and utility setups. The challenge is not just in fitting these pieces together but also in doing so in a way that aligns with your financial landscape. This chapter is about transforming that financial jigsaw into a clear, cohesive picture, ensuring no piece goes unnoticed and your dream build doesn't turn into a budgetary nightmare.

Setting a Realistic Budget for Your Barndominium Dream

Cost Breakdown

Let's start by laying all the pieces on the table. Building a barndominium involves a myriad of costs, and understanding each one is key to setting a realistic budget. Let's get you started with a breakdown:

- **Land Acquisition**: The foundation of your project, both literally and figuratively. Prices vary widely based on location, size, and accessibility.
- **Construction Costs**: From framing to finishing touches, this will likely be your largest expense. Factors like materials, labor, and the complexity of your design play significant roles.
- **Permits and Legal Fees**: Often overlooked, but crucial for keeping your project on the right side of the law.
- **Utilities and Infrastructure**: Think about the costs of providing water, electricity, sewage, and internet to your barndominium, especially if your site is in a remote location.
- **Interior and Exterior Finishes**: The details that transform a structure into a home. This includes everything from cabinets and countertops to siding and roofing.
- **Landscaping**: Setting aside funds for basic landscaping will ensure your barndominium isn't a diamond in the rough.

Budgeting Strategies

With a clear understanding of the costs, it's time to match them with your financial picture. Here are some strategies:

- **Prioritize Your Needs**: Separate your must-haves from your nice-to-haves. Essentials get budgeted first.
- **Set Aside a Contingency Fund**: Unexpected costs are part

of the process. A contingency fund of 10-20% of your total budget is a safety net you'll be glad to have.

- **Phase Your Project**: If funds are tight, consider phasing your project. Start with the essentials and add on as your budget allows.

Financial Planning Resources

To keep your finances in check, leverage the following tools designed for the job:

- **Budgeting Software**: Apps like Mint or YNAB (You Need A Budget) can help you track expenses and manage your money more effectively.
- **Loan Calculators**: Planning to finance your project? Online calculators can help you understand loan costs over time.
- **Budget Tracker Template**: Use a simple Excel spreadsheet or Google Sheets to keep a tab on expenses as they arise. This helps with real-time tracking and ensures you stay within your financial bounds.

Money-Saving Tips

Finally, let's talk about stretching those dollars without compromising your vision:

- **Shop around for Materials**: Prices can vary significantly between suppliers. Don't shy away from negotiating for better deals or exploring reclaimed and recycled materials. In addition to being cost-effective, they can add aesthetic quality to your home.

- **Do It Yourself (Where You Can):** Certain tasks, such as painting, installing fixtures, or even laying tile, can be DIYed with a bit of research and patience, saving you labor costs.
- **Hire Wisely:** For tasks beyond your skill set, hiring the right professionals can actually save money in the long run by avoiding costly mistakes. Do your research and interview multiple contractors.

Building a barndominium is as much about financial planning as it is about construction. By understanding all potential costs, employing smart budgeting strategies, utilizing resources, and applying money-saving tips, you can create a financial plan that brings your barndominium to life without breaking the bank.

Choosing the Right Property for Your Barndominium

Unless you are converting an existing building, finding the perfect spot for your barndominium is like searching for a needle in a haystack, except this needle can significantly shape your future living experience. The thrill of the hunt is real, and so are the considerations that come with it. It's not just about the view or the size; it's about how the land aligns with your vision for a barndominium that's as functional as it is beautiful. Let's peel back the layers of what makes a property right for you.

Location Considerations

The saying "location, location, location" holds a new meaning when it comes to a barndominium. This choice impacts not just your daily life but also the design and functionality of your future home. A serene spot in the countryside might offer the idyllic setting you crave, but consider how it affects your commute, access to amenities, and social life. On the flip side, a location closer to a town might sacrifice some of that tranquility for convenience. The key here is balance; find a spot that harmonizes with your lifestyle, allowing your barndominium to be a retreat without feeling isolated.

Land Evaluation

Before falling in love with a piece of land, give it a thorough evaluation to ensure it's suited for your barndominium. Start with zoning laws; they dictate what you can and cannot build, and running afoul of them can halt your project before it starts. Next, scrutinize the topography. A sloped lot might offer stunning views but could also escalate construction costs. Similarly, the soil type can affect the foundation work required. Don't overlook access to utilities, either. If the land isn't already connected to power, water, and sewage systems, the costs of doing so can add up quickly. A good rule of thumb is to consult with an engineer or surveyor who can provide insights into these aspects.

Future Development

While you might be drawn to a location for its current charm, it's wise to consider what the future holds. Areas poised for development could see an increase in traffic, noise, and neighbors, potentially impacting the tranquil setting you initially enjoyed. Conversely, development can also mean enhanced infrastructure and amenities, potentially increasing your property's value. Investigating the local area's development plans gives you a glimpse into the future, helping you make an informed decision that aligns with your long-term vision for your barndominium.

Legal and Environmental Checks

Digging into the legal and environmental history of a property is a must-do that can save you from future headaches. Start with a title search to ensure the land is free of liens or disputes. This ensures that legal snags won't hold you back when you're ready to build. Environmental checks are equally important. Look for any signs of contamination from previous uses that could pose health risks or require costly cleanup. Wetlands, endangered species habitats, flood zones, or areas prone to wildfires are other environmental factors that could restrict your building plans or necessitate additional permits as well as increased insurance costs in the future. Seeking out information from the U.S. Geological Society or engaging an environmental consultant to conduct these checks might seem like an extra step, but it's a move that can safeguard your investment and your vision.

Choosing the right property for your barndominium is a journey that intertwines dreams with due diligence. It's about seeing beyond the surface, asking the right questions, and making choices that resonate with your vision for a home. This process not only ensures that your barndominium stands on solid ground, both literally and figuratively, but also that it's a place where your future can flourish.

Navigating Zoning Laws and Building Permits

When it's time to turn your barndominium dreams into reality, understanding and adhering to local zoning laws and obtaining the necessary building permits are steps that cannot be overlooked. These regulations are in place to ensure that your new home is safe, sustainable, and in harmony with its surroundings.

Let's break down how to approach these often complex but crucial aspects of your project.

Researching Local Regulations

First things first, you'll need to get familiar with the zoning laws and building codes specific to your area. These regulations govern what can be built, where it can be built, and how it must be constructed. They can vary widely from one municipality to another, so it's important to gather information that's specific to your location. Here's how you can start:

- **Visit Your Local Zoning Office**: This should be one of your first stops. The staff there can provide you with the zoning regulations that apply to your property and offer guidance on how to comply.
- **Check Online Resources**: Many local governments have zoning maps and building codes available on their websites. These can be a good starting point for understanding the rules that apply to your project.
- **Consult with a Builder or General Contractor**: Talk with a builder or general contractor who is familiar with local building codes and zoning laws. They can provide valuable insight into the specific regulations that will affect your project.
- **Consult with Neighbors**: Sometimes, the best insights come from those who have gone through the process themselves. Chat with neighbors who have undertaken construction projects to learn from their experiences.

Permit Application Process

Securing a building permit is a step that officially allows you to start construction. The process can seem daunting, but breaking it down makes it more manageable. Here's what you typically need to do:

- **Gather Necessary Documents**: This usually includes detailed plans of your barndominium, including architectural designs and site plans. You might also need to submit proof of property ownership and any relevant permits, such as for septic systems or wells.
- **Submit Your Application**: Once you have all your documents in order, submit them to your local building department. There's often a fee associated with the application, which can vary based on the size and complexity of your project.
- **Wait for Review**: After submission, your plans will be reviewed to ensure they comply with local codes. This can take anywhere from a few weeks to a few months, depending on the backlog at your local office.
- **Address Any Issues**: If there are any problems with your plans, you'll need to address these and resubmit. This might require making modifications to your design or providing additional information.
- **Receive Your Permit**: Once your plans are approved, you'll receive your building permit, and you can officially begin construction.

Facing Challenges

It's not uncommon to run into hurdles when dealing with zoning laws or the permit application process. Here's how you can handle potential issues:

- **Seek Variances or Amendments**: If your project doesn't comply with existing zoning laws, you may need to apply for a variance or amendment. This is essentially a request to deviate from the rules, and it usually requires proving that your project won't negatively impact the community.
- **Be Proactive about Communication**: Keeping an open line of communication with your local zoning office can help you navigate challenges more smoothly. Don't hesitate to ask questions or seek clarification on any issues that arise.

When to Get Professional Help

Sometimes, the complexities of zoning laws and permit applications warrant bringing in a professional. Here's when you should consider it:

- **Complex Projects**: If your barndominium involves unusual designs or is located in an area with strict regulations, a professional can help ensure everything is up to code.
- **Legal Challenges**: If you're facing legal obstacles, such as disputes over land use, a lawyer who specializes in real estate or land use law can be invaluable.
- **Navigating Bureaucracy**: An experienced architect or builder can offer assistance with the permit application

process, particularly with navigating the requirements and red tape.

Navigating zoning laws and building permits is a critical step in bringing your barndominium to life. While it can sometimes feel like you're jumping through hoops, remember that these regulations are designed to ensure that your home is safe, sustainable, and a positive addition to the community. With careful research, patience, and perhaps a bit of professional help, you can navigate these waters successfully, laying the groundwork for your dream barndominium.

Designing Your Barndominium: Blending Functionality With Aesthetics

Designing a barndominium calls for a balanced approach where aesthetics meet functionality. It's a process that invites you to pour your dreams and practical needs into a mold, shaping a living space that not only looks splendid but also fits your lifestyle like a glove. This section navigates through setting design goals, the advantages of collaboration, tapping into various inspiration wells, and the joy of sprinkling personal touches throughout your home.

Defining Your Design Goals

Imagine your barndominium as a tapestry, each thread representing an element of your life. The colors and patterns should not only please the eye but also weave seamlessly into the fabric of your daily routines. Start by listing what matters most to you in a home. Is it the efficiency of the space, the warmth it radiates, or perhaps its capability to host gatherings? Maybe it's a quiet corner for your morning coffee or a spacious workshop for your creative outbursts. Aligning these priorities early on ensures your design serves you on a functional level while satisfying your aesthetic appetite. Consider how each room will be used, who will use it, and what mood you wish to create. This clarity acts as a North Star, guiding your design decisions.

Collaboration with Designers

Diving into the design phase with a professional can turn your vision into a detailed plan that ticks all the boxes. Architects and designers bring a wealth of knowledge and experience, especially those familiar with barndominiums. They understand how to maximize space, light, and energy efficiency while navigating the technicalities of building codes. Their expertise can elevate your design, introducing elements you might not have considered, such as innovative storage solutions or eco-friendly materials. Moreover, they serve as a bridge between your vision and the construction team, ensuring the final outcome mirrors your initial concept. Remember, a good designer listens, adapts, and collaborates, making your dream home a shared goal.

Design Inspiration Sources

With the world at our fingertips, inspiration is never far away. It's about knowing where to look. Architectural magazines, both in print and online, are treasure troves of ideas, showcasing the latest trends, timeless designs, and innovative solutions. Websites like Houzz or Pinterest allow you to create virtual mood boards, collecting images that spark creativity. Don't overlook the value of home design shows; they not only present design concepts but also delve into the challenges and solutions encountered during the building process. Online forums dedicated to barndominiums can also offer a wealth of real-life inspiration and advice from those who've walked the path before you.

Incorporating Personal Touches

The essence of a home lies in its ability to reflect the personalities of those who live within its walls. This is where your barndominium can truly shine. Start with elements that hold sentimental value, be they a family heirloom or artwork collected on your travels. These pieces can serve as focal points around which rooms are designed. Consider custom-built features that cater to your hobbies or lifestyle, from a sunlit reading nook to a robust garage workshop. The choice of colors, textures, and materials also plays a significant role in personalizing your space. Opt for those that evoke positive emotions or memories. Remember, this is your canvas; don't be afraid to leave your mark. Whether it's through a bold accent wall, a handmade light fixture, or a custom-tiled back-splash, these personal touches infuse your barndominium with character and warmth, making it unmistakably yours.

Designing your barndominium is a journey that intertwines dreams with practicality, weaving a living space that resonates on a personal level while meeting day-to-day needs. Through a blend of clear goals, professional collaboration, diverse sources of inspiration, and uniquely personal elements, your barndominium becomes more than just a structure. It transforms into a sanctuary that reflects your personality, embraces your lifestyle, and stands as a testament to your vision brought to life.

Assembling Your Barndominium Building Team: Tips for Hiring Contractors

Selecting the right crew to bring your barndominium from a sketch on paper to a standing testament of your vision is no small feat. It's akin to casting for a blockbuster movie; every role is pivotal. Here, the aim is to guide you through the process of creating a team that not only understands your vision but also possesses the skills and integrity to execute it flawlessly.

Finding the Right Professionals

The quest for the perfect building team starts with knowing where to look. Recommendations from friends or family who have undertaken similar projects can be gold. Local builders' associations and online platforms dedicated to home construction and design also offer directories of professionals with a range of expertise. When your search is underway, keep an eye out for those who have experience specifically with barndominiums. Their familiarity with the unique aspects of these structures can make a significant difference in navigating the challenges that may arise during construction.

Interviewing Potential Hires

Once you have a shortlist, the interview process begins. Think of it as not just assessing their skills but also determining if they're a good fit for your team. Consider asking:

- What experience do you have with barndominiums or similar projects?
- Can you provide a detailed timeline and budget estimate for a project like mine?
- How do you handle unexpected challenges or delays?
- What's your communication style and frequency with clients during a project?
- Can you share examples of how you've incorporated clients' custom design elements into past projects?
- These questions aim to gauge not only their technical

ability but also their problem-solving skills, reliability, and commitment to client satisfaction.

Evaluate their professionalism. Does he/she present himself/herself as a business owner? Are they on time for appointments and prompt with replies to texts or calls? Do they seem organized? This is a reflection of how your project will be managed, so it is beneficial to pay attention.

Checking References and Past Work

Now, for the detective work. Digging into a professional's past projects and speaking to former clients offers invaluable insights into their work ethic and the quality of their craftsmanship. Request a portfolio of their work, focusing on projects similar to yours. When checking references, ask about the contractor's punctuality, transparency, response to feedback, and whether the project stayed on budget and schedule. Check with the local Better Business Bureau or sites like Home Advisor to look for any complaints logged or issued. Also, verify they are licensed, bonded, and insured; this guarantees they meet all legal requirements to undertake your project. This step is crucial to building confidence in your choice and ensuring your project is in capable hands.

Contract Negotiation

With the right team in place, the next step is to make it official through contracts. This legal agreement should detail every aspect of the project, from scope and timelines to payment schedules and materials used. Here are a few pointers for a smooth negotiation:

- Ensure the contract includes a detailed description of the work to be done, the materials to be used, and the expected timeframe for completion.
- Agree on a payment schedule that aligns with project milestones and be wary of any requests for large upfront payments.
- Include clauses that outline how changes to the original plan, including adjustments to costs and timelines, will be handled.
- Discuss warranties and what they cover. It's important to know you're protected should anything not meet the agreed-upon standards.

This legal groundwork not only sets clear expectations for both parties but also provides a roadmap that helps keep the project on course.

As we close this chapter, remember that assembling your barndominium building team is a step that demands diligence, patience, and clear communication. From the initial search to the final handshake, every decision you make shapes the journey of creating a home that's a true reflection of your vision and values. With the right professionals by your side, you're well-equipped to navigate the complexities of construction, transform challenges into triumphs, and breathe life into your barndominium.

Moving forward, the focus shifts from planning and preparation to action. The next chapter will delve into the nuts and bolts of construction, guiding you through laying a solid foundation, erecting sturdy walls, and adding those finishing touches that make a house a home. With your team in place and plans at the ready, it's time to turn those blueprints into reality.

THREE

Architectural Design and Planning

Imagine standing at a crossroads, one path lined with pre-fabricated kits, the other meandering through custom design blueprints. This isn't just about choosing how to build a barndominium; it's about deciding how much of your personal touch you want to infuse into your future home. Both routes have their allure, their challenges, and their rewards. Let's unpack the pros and cons of custom plans versus kit barndominiums, guiding you to make a choice that resonates with your lifestyle, budget, and timeline.

Customization Levels

- **Custom Plans**: Have you ever dreamt of a kitchen that caters precisely to your culinary adventures or a workshop with just the right amount of space for your projects? Custom plans turn these dreams into blueprints. Here, every nook is yours to design, ensuring your barndominium mirrors your lifestyle down to the smallest detail. The sky's the limit, but so is the requirement for decision-making.

- **Kit Barndominiums**: Picture a kit as a high-quality puzzle; the pieces are predetermined, but the final picture still has your touch. These kits offer a range of layouts and styles, providing a balance between customization and convenience. While you might not decide where every outlet goes, you can still choose finishes that reflect your style.

Cost Implications

- **Custom Plans**: Delving into custom designs typically entails a higher upfront cost. You're not just paying for materials but also for professional design services. However, this route allows you to tailor your home to be energy-efficient, potentially saving you a bundle on utility bills in the long run. Plus, custom plans can be adapted to your budget, prioritizing features that offer the most bang for your buck.
- **Kit Barndominiums**: Generally more wallet-friendly at the outset, kits streamline the construction process, potentially reducing labor costs. However, the fixed nature of a kit might result in compromises or additions that could inflate the total cost. It's a bit like buying a base model car and then paying extra for every upgrade.

Time Considerations

- **Custom Plans**: Patience is key. Crafting a home that's a perfect fit for your needs takes time, not just in the design phase but also through careful selection of materials and builders who can bring your vision to life. Think of it as slow-cooking a gourmet meal; the preparation might be lengthy, but the result is worth the wait.

- **Kit Barndominiums**: If you're looking to move in sooner rather than later, kits can fast-track the process. With pre-designed plans and materials ready to go, construction can begin much quicker. It's akin to assembling a high-end BBQ grill; follow the instructions, and you'll be cooking in no time.

Quality and Durability

- **Custom Plans**: When you go custom, you call the shots on materials, ensuring each component meets your standards for durability and aesthetics. This control can lead to a home that not only looks exactly as you envisioned but is also built to stand the test of time.
- **Kit Barndominiums**: The quality of a kit can vary by manufacturer, but reputable providers use materials that ensure your home is safe and sturdy. It's important to research and choose a kit from a company known for its quality, much like selecting a car based on the manufacturer's reputation for reliability and performance.

Choosing between custom plans and kit barndominiums boils down to a few key factors: how much personalization you crave, your budget, your timeline, and the importance you place on quality and durability. As you weigh these options, consider not just the home you want to build today but also the life you want to live in it for years to come. Whether you decide on a kit that offers ease and efficiency or embark on the journey of custom design for a truly one-of-a-kind home, the path you choose will lead to a place that's uniquely yours.

Maximizing Space and Efficiency in Your Barndominium

In the quest to craft a barndominium that's as functional as it is stylish, space planning emerges as a critical piece of the puzzle. This isn't just about ensuring that your furniture fits; it's about designing a home that adapts to your life's rhythms, effortlessly accommodating both the bustling moments and the quiet pauses. Here's how you can make every inch of your barndominium work for you, creating spaces that are both versatile and inviting.

Space Planning

Strategic space planning starts with a clear understanding of your daily routines and how you envision using different areas of your home. It's about foreseeing the flow from one activity to the next and crafting spaces that facilitate this movement. Consider, for example, the path from your bedroom to your morning coffee spot. Is it straightforward, or does it require navigating through less-used spaces? The goal is to create logical, accessible paths within your home that align with your habits.

- **Zoning**: Divide your barndominium into zones based on activity—for instance, sleeping, dining, working, and relaxation zones. This helps allocate space effectively and set the right mood in each area.
- **Flexibility**: Design spaces that can easily adapt to different needs. A dining area might double as a workspace during the day. Flexible, open layouts allow you to redefine spaces as your requirements evolve.

Multi-Functional Areas

The beauty of a barndominium is in its ability to host a variety of life scenarios under one roof. Here are examples of multi-functional design solutions that epitomize this adaptability:

- **Office/Guest Room**: A well-designed office that doubles as a guest room can be a game-changer. Think Murphy beds that fold away when not needed or a sleek sofa bed paired with a desk that can be tucked away.
- **Kitchen Islands with a Twist**: An island can be more than just a prep area. With the right design, it can serve as a casual dining spot, a homework station for kids, or even a makeshift office space.

Energy Efficiency

Incorporating energy efficiency into your design not only lowers utility bills but also contributes to a healthier planet. Here's how you can weave energy efficiency into the fabric of your barndominium:

- **Insulation**: Proper insulation is the cornerstone of energy-efficient design. It keeps your home warm in the winter and cool in the summer, reducing the need for artificial heating and cooling.
- **Smart Systems**: From programmable thermostats to energy-efficient HVAC systems, technology offers myriad ways to cut down on energy consumption. Smart systems adapt to your lifestyle, ensuring that you're using energy only when you need it.

Natural Lighting and Ventilation

- **Balance**: The right balance of light and air can transform the feel of a space, making it more welcoming and healthier to live in. Here's how to bring the benefits of the outdoors into your barndominium:
- **Window Placement**: Position windows to maximize natural light throughout the day, reducing the need for artificial lighting. Large, south-facing windows can help warm your home in the colder months.
- **Cross Ventilation**: Allow for cross ventilation by placing windows on opposite sides of a room. This natural air flow keeps your home cool and fresh without relying solely on air conditioning.
- **Skylights and Solar Tubes**: For areas where traditional windows might not be feasible, consider skylights or solar tubes. They funnel natural light into the heart of your home, brightening up spaces without compromising privacy.

In weaving together these elements of space planning, multifunctionality, energy efficiency, and natural lighting, you're not just building a barndominium. You're crafting a living environment that moves with you, breathes with you, and evolves with you. It's about creating a backdrop for your life that's as dynamic and vibrant as the memories you'll make within its walls.

Incorporating Sustainability into Your Design

Building a barndominium that nods to sustainability is like crafting a love letter to the environment. It's about choosing materials and methods that respect the earth while creating a space that's as beautiful as it is eco-conscious. This section explores how to weave sustainability into every fiber of your barndominium from the ground up.

Sustainable Materials

Opting for eco-friendly building materials is a significant step toward a greener home. These choices not only minimize environmental impact but often come with added benefits like improved indoor air quality and reduced energy costs. Here are a few examples:

- **Bamboo Flooring**: Celebrated for its rapid renewability, bamboo offers a durable and stylish flooring option. Its versatility in design and color can complement any aesthetic, from modern chic to rustic charm.
- **Recycled Metal Roofing**: Metal roofs made from recycled materials provide longevity and energy efficiency. They reflect sunlight, helping to keep your barndominium cooler in the summer months.
- **Reclaimed Wood**: Using reclaimed wood for beams, flooring, or accents not only adds character and warmth to your space but also reduces the demand for new lumber. Each piece tells a story, adding a layer of history to your home.
- **Low-VOC Paints and Finishes**: Selecting paints and finishes with low volatile organic compounds (VOCs) improves indoor air quality, ensuring your home is as healthy as it is beautiful.

Renewable Energy Options

Harnessing the power of renewable energy is a game-changer for reducing your barndominium's carbon footprint. Here's how you can integrate these technologies:

- **Solar Panels**: Installing solar panels can significantly reduce reliance on grid electricity. Opt for a rooftop system or ground-mounted panels, depending on your property's layout and sun exposure.
- **Geothermal Heating and Cooling**: This system uses the earth's stable underground temperature to heat and cool your home efficiently. While the upfront cost can be higher, the long-term savings and environmental benefits are substantial.
- **Wind Turbines**: If your property is in a windy area, small-scale wind turbines can provide an additional renewable energy source, further decreasing your reliance on fossil fuels.

Water Conservation

Mindful water use is crucial to building a sustainable home. Implement these strategies to conserve water:

- **Rainwater Harvesting Systems**: Collect rainwater for landscaping, flushing toilets, and even laundry. This system reduces demand for municipal water supplies and can lead to significant savings.
- **Water-Efficient Fixtures**: Faucets, showers, and toilets that are designed to use less water without sacrificing performance are key to reducing your overall water consumption. Look for products with the EPA's WaterSense label for maximum efficiency.

Landscaping and Outdoor Spaces

The space surrounding your barndominium offers a prime opportunity to support local ecosystems while enhancing the beauty of your property. Consider these landscaping practices:

- **Native Plants**: Filling your garden with native plants reduces water usage and provides habitat for local wildlife. These plants are adapted to your climate, requiring less maintenance and no chemical fertilizers.
- **Permeable Paving**: Opt for permeable materials for driveways and walkways to allow rainwater to recharge groundwater rather than run off into storm drains.
- **Edible Gardens**: Incorporating vegetable patches and fruit trees not only provides fresh produce but also contributes to local food security and reduces the carbon footprint associated with transporting food.
- **Green Roofs and Walls**: If you're feeling adventurous, green roofs and living walls offer insulation, reduce stormwater runoff, and create habitats for birds and insects.

Incorporating sustainability into your barndominium design isn't just about making eco-friendly choices; it's about creating a home that exists in harmony with its environment. It's a commitment to a lifestyle that values resourcefulness, efficiency, and a deep respect for the natural world. Through thoughtful selection of materials, integration of renewable energy, water conservation efforts, and sustainable landscaping practices, your barndominium can stand as a testament to what's possible when we build with the future in mind.

Selecting Materials: Durability Meets Style

When it comes to creating a barndominium that will stand the test of time while looking like something out of your Pinterest board, picking the right materials is key. This phase is where practicality meets aesthetics, and together, they decide on the elements that will make up your future home. Let's break down the nitty-gritty of choosing materials that balance durability, style, and sustainability.

Material Selection Criteria

Picking out materials is like setting up dominoes; each choice impacts the next, influencing the overall look, feel, and longevity of your home. Here's what to keep in mind:

- **Durability**: The materials should be tough enough to withstand both the elements and the daily wear and tear of life. Think about your location and the climate in your area. Will the materials stand up to scorching sun, whipping winds, or relentless rain?
- **Aesthetic Appeal**: The look of the materials is just as important as their strength. You want materials that sing in harmony with your envisioned style, whether that's rustic chic, industrial edge, or minimalist modern.
- **Sustainability**: With an eye on the future, opt for materials that do little harm to our planet. Renewable resources, recycled content, and energy-efficient options should be at the top of your list.
- **Local Availability**: Materials that are locally sourced not only reduce transportation emissions but often blend seamlessly with the local landscape and style.

Cost vs. Value

Navigating the balance between cost and value requires a keen eye and a bit of foresight. It's easy to gravitate toward cheaper options, but investing in higher-quality materials can save money in the long run through reduced maintenance and energy costs. For example, high-performance windows might pinch the wallet initially, but the amount they save in heating and cooling costs over the years will make them worth their weight in gold.

Maintenance Considerations

The dream of living in a barndominium comes with the reality of upkeep. Consider how much maintenance you're willing to commit to when selecting materials. Some materials might look stunning and fit your budget, but they require constant care to keep them looking their best. For instance:

- **Metal Roofing**: Offers durability with minimal upkeep, lasting decades without needing much more than an occasional rinse.
- **Composite Decking**: Mimics the warmth of wood without the hassle of yearly staining or sealing.

Opting for materials that promise longevity with minimal maintenance allows you to spend more time enjoying your home rather than laboring over it.

Material Sourcing

Finding the right materials involves a mix of detective work and networking. Here are some avenues to explore:

- **Reclaimed and Recycled**: Salvage yards and specialty suppliers often stock a treasure trove of reclaimed wood, metal, and stone. Not only do these materials add instant character and history to your home, but they also reduce the demand for new resources.
- **Local Suppliers**: Supporting local businesses not only bolsters the community but can also offer advantages in

terms of materials that are well-suited to the local climate and style. Plus, the suppliers are a wellspring of knowledge on what works best in your area.

- **Sustainable Sources**: For new materials, look for suppliers who prioritize sustainability. This could mean anything from sourcing lumber from responsibly managed forests to offering products made with recycled content.

Selecting materials is one of the most impactful steps in building a barndominium. It's where you decide not just on the visual and tactile elements that will define your space but also on the environmental footprint and practical aspects of your home. By choosing wisely, you set the stage for a home that's not only a feast for the eyes but also a fortress against the elements and a friend to the planet.

Achieving the Ideal Indoor-Outdoor Flow

Crafting a space that seamlessly unites the indoors with the outdoors is like directing a grand performance where nature takes center stage. This seamless blend not only magnifies the beauty of your barndominium but also elevates the everyday living experience. It invites the outdoors in and encourages life to spill gracefully outside, blurring the lines between constructed spaces and natural serenity.

Design Principles for Flow: The Magic Lies in the Details

- Large sliding doors or bi-folds act as a gateway, not just in a physical sense but visually, too, extending the living space into the outdoors with elegance.
- Consistent flooring materials that stretch from inside to

outside create an unbroken line of sight, making both areas feel like one cohesive space.

- The strategic use of glass, not just in doors but as walls, can further dissolve barriers, allowing you to gaze out at rolling hills or lush gardens from the comfort of your sofa.

Outdoor Living Spaces: Where Imagination Meets Relaxation

- Patios become second living rooms on sunny days, perfect for morning coffees or evening wind-downs. Deck them out with comfy seating, add a fire pit for warmth, and you've got an all-season retreat.
- Outdoor kitchens take dining al fresco to a new level. Whether it's summer barbecues or cozy autumn dinners, these spaces invite gatherings, conversations, and culinary adventures under the open sky.
- Pergolas and gazebos not only provide shelter but also define outdoor rooms without boxing them in, offering a shaded haven to enjoy the fresh air.

Landscaping Integration

Nature plays its part beautifully, connecting the built environment with the natural world like a picture book.

- Softscaping, with lush lawns, flower beds, and shrubbery, creates a visual and tactile softness that contrasts yet complements the hard lines of architectural elements.
- Hardscaping, like stone paths or wooden decks, guides movement and invites exploration, leading the way from indoors to out.
- Water features, be they a small pond, a fountain, or a pool,

add a dynamic element to the garden, and their sounds and movements bring tranquility and a sense of renewal.

Views and Privacy

Find the right balance between celebrating views and cherishing privacy.

- Strategic window placement allows you to capture the best vistas without compromising on seclusion. Think picture windows in a secluded spot or skylights that open up to the sky without giving away anything to prying eyes.
- Privacy screens, whether built as part of the architecture or incorporated into the landscaping with tall hedges or climbing plants, shield your haven from the outside world while adding an element of beauty.
- Orientation plays a crucial role, too. Positioning living spaces to face private views or creating secluded outdoor nooks ensures you can enjoy the beauty of your surroundings without feeling exposed.

In weaving together these elements of design, outdoor living, landscaping, and careful consideration of views and privacy, you're not just building a home. You're crafting an experience, a place where every day feels like a dialogue with the natural world. It's about creating spaces that invite you to live not just in them but with them, in harmony with the rhythms of nature and the flow of life.

As we wrap up this exploration into blending indoor and outdoor living, remember that the beauty of a barndominium lies in its versatility, its ability to become whatever you need it to be. From the materials you choose to the way you integrate nature into your living spaces, every decision is a step toward creating a home that's not just a place to live but a way to live. Up next, we'll delve into the heart of the home—the interior design and personalization that make it uniquely yours.

FOUR

Interior Design Mastery – Making Your Barndominium a Reflection of You

Picture walking into a space that immediately feels like home. The colors, the textures, the layout—everything just clicks, resonating with your personal style and lifestyle needs. That's the power of masterful interior design, especially in a barndominium where traditional and modern elements blend to create something truly unique. This chapter is about turning that vision into your everyday reality, making your barndominium not just a place to live but a vibrant canvas of your personal journey.

Defining Your Interior Style

Before diving into paint swatches or furniture catalogs, take a moment to really think about what makes you tick. Your home should be a reflection of your personality, interests, and lifestyle. Are you drawn to the sleek lines and neutral palette of minimalism, or does the warmth and eclectic nature of bohemian style speak to you? Maybe you're somewhere in between, craving the rustic warmth of farmhouse chic with a hint of industrial edge.

- **Start with a Mood Board**: Collect images, fabrics, and even objects that inspire you. Tools like Pinterest can be invaluable for this.
- **Consider Your Lifestyle**: Your day-to-day life should guide your style choices. A home office might need a more focused, serene setup, while a family living area might prioritize comfort and durability.
- **Mix, Don't Match**: It's okay to blend styles. The contrast between a sleek modern sofa and a rustic wood coffee table can add depth and interest to your space.

Space Utilization

One of the joys of barndominium living is the generous space it offers, especially with open-concept layouts. However, large, open spaces can feel overwhelming if not thoughtfully planned.

- **Zones Are Your Friends**: Use furniture, rugs, or even lighting to define different areas within a larger space. A reading nook by a window or a gaming corner can carve out personal retreats within the home. And don't forget to factor in foot traffic when you are planning your zones so that the flow through your home is not impeded.
- **Lofted Areas**: If your barndominium includes high ceilings, consider adding a loft. It can serve as an extra bedroom, an office, or a cozy lounge area, making use of vertical space.
- **Open Yet Organized**: Open shelves can divide areas while providing display space for books, plants, or collectibles, adding personality without the bulk of walls or large furniture.

Color Schemes and Textures

Colors and textures bring a space to life, adding layers of visual interest and emotional warmth.

- **Start with a Neutral Base**: Especially in open-concept areas, starting with a neutral palette for walls and large furniture items can create a cohesive look. Then, add pops of color with accessories like cushions, rugs, or art.
- **Play with Texture**: Mix materials to keep things interesting. Combine soft textiles with harder materials like wood or metal. A chunky knit throw on a leather couch or velvet cushions on a sleek metal chair can create a dynamic look.
- **Reflect Your Surroundings**: Draw inspiration from the landscape around your barndominium. Forested areas might inspire earthy greens and browns, while a desert setting might lean toward warm oranges and reds.

Personalization Tips

The final layer in making your barndominium truly yours is personalization. This is where your unique story comes into play.

- **Display What You Love**: Whether it's art, photographs, or souvenirs from travels, let your passions be visible. Open shelving or gallery walls can turn your memories into decor.
- **DIY Projects**: Adding your own touch through DIY projects can be both fun and fulfilling. Upcycle an old piece of furniture, create a piece of art, or build a custom bookshelf.

- **Unique Finds**: Flea markets, antique stores, and even online marketplaces can be goldmines for one-of-a-kind pieces that add character and history to your home.

Remember, the goal is to create a space that resonates with you on every level. From the overarching style down to the smallest detail, every choice is an opportunity to reflect who you are and how you live. Your barndominium is a blank canvas—have fun painting it with the colors of your life.

Creative Solutions for Storage and Organization

In the realm of barndominium living, where the beauty of vast, open spaces meets the challenge of keeping everything in its place, innovative storage solutions become not just helpful but transformative. Here, the aim is to maintain that open, airy feel while ensuring every item has a home, making your space both beautiful and functional.

Innovative Storage Solutions

In the quest for organization, thinking outside the traditional storage box opens up a world of possibilities. Consider wall-mounted systems that allow for customization and flexibility, letting you adjust shelves, hooks, and compartments to suit your evolving needs. Magnetic panels in the kitchen or workshop keep tools and utensils within reach yet out of the way. For items best kept out of sight, stylish storage ottomans or benches offer dual functionality, providing a place to sit as well as stash away blankets, games, or seasonal decor.

Built-In Storage

The integration of built-in storage solutions can significantly enhance the functionality of your barndominium without sacrificing its design aesthetic. Custom shelving built into alcoves or along empty wall spaces creates room for books, display items, and more, ensuring that these items add to the decor rather than clutter it. Window seats with under-seat storage not only offer a cozy spot for reading but also additional space for linens or seldom-used kitchenware. In bedrooms, consider a platform bed with drawers underneath, maximizing the use of space while maintaining a clean, uncluttered look.

Multi-Purpose Furniture

Furniture that serves more than one purpose is a game-changer in any home, but especially in a barndominium where blending functionality with style is key. A dining table that extends offers a compact solution for daily use while providing the option to accommodate guests when entertaining. Sofa beds in the living area or office ensure that your barndominium can easily welcome overnight guests without the need for a dedicated guest room. Look for coffee tables with hidden storage or modular sofas that can be reconfigured to suit different occasions and needs.

Organizational Systems

A well-organized barndominium is the result of thoughtfully chosen organizational systems that cater to the specifics of your lifestyle. Closet organizers with adjustable shelving, rods, and drawers ensure that every garment or accessory has its place, making the most of vertical space and keeping wardrobes tidy. In the kitchen, pull-out pantries, spice racks, and under-sink organizers optimize storage and accessibility. Embracing digital home management apps can also revolutionize how you organize, allowing you to keep track of everything from grocery lists to maintenance schedules in one easily accessible place.

Incorporating these storage and organization solutions ensures your barndominium remains a sanctuary of calm and order amid the whirlwind of daily life. By choosing options that blend seamlessly with the aesthetics of your home while addressing practical needs, you create a space that's not only beautiful to look at but also a joy to live in.

Choosing the Right Finishes for Your Barndominium: Floors, Walls, and Ceilings

In the heart of every barndominium, the finishes you select for floors, walls, and ceilings do more than just cover surfaces. They set the stage for your home's ambiance, echoing your unique flair while ensuring every room is clad in durability and comfort. This section delves into navigating these choices, ensuring you strike the perfect balance between form and function.

Flooring Options

Selecting the right flooring is pivotal for any home, but in a barndominium, where the blend of rustic and modern is often a key theme, it becomes even more crucial. Here's a look at some popular options:

- **Concrete**: Known for their sturdiness and ease of maintenance, polished concrete floors offer a sleek, industrial look. They excel in high-traffic areas but can be cold underfoot if not paired with radiant heating.

- **Hardwood**: Nothing beats the warmth and timeless appeal of hardwood. It's durable and versatile enough to match any decor style. However, it requires more maintenance to keep it looking its best.
- **Tile**: Ceramic or porcelain tiles are excellent for moisture-prone areas like kitchens and bathrooms. Available in a vast array of designs, they can mimic the look of wood or stone. The downside? They can be cold and hard underfoot.
- **Laminate**: A cost-effective alternative to hardwood, laminate flooring is easy to install and maintain. While it mimics the look of natural wood quite well, it doesn't offer the same longevity or feel.
- **Luxury Vinyl Tile**: A modern flooring solution that combines the beauty of natural materials with the resilience and versatility of vinyl. It's known for its ability to closely mimic the look of hardwood, stone, or ceramic tiles while providing enhanced durability and moisture resistance. Ideal for areas with high foot traffic or potential spills, LVT is easy to clean and maintain. Despite its toughness, it offers a softer, warmer underfoot experience compared to traditional tile or stone, making it a comfortable choice for any room.

Each of these flooring options brings its own set of benefits and considerations. Weighing them against your lifestyle and the overall aesthetic of your barndominium will guide you to the perfect choice.

Wall Treatments and Textures

Walls are your home's canvas, and the way you choose to finish them can dramatically alter the space's character. Here are some ideas to consider:

- **Exposed Brick**: For a touch of industrial charm or rustic warmth, leaving brick walls exposed can add depth and texture to your space. This works well in achieving a loft-style look or a cozy country vibe.
- **Wood Paneling**: Whether you opt for reclaimed wood for a rustic feel or sleek, painted panels for a more contemporary look, wood adds warmth and texture to any room. It's versatile and can be used as an accent or throughout a whole room.
- **Modern Plaster Techniques**: Smooth plaster walls with a polished finish can bring a modern, sophisticated feel to your barndominium. Adding color tints directly to the plaster can create a rich, velvety texture that paint alone cannot achieve.

Incorporating these textures isn't just about aesthetics; it's about creating a tactile experience that enriches your daily living environment.

Ceiling Design

The design of your ceiling has a profound impact on the perception of space within your barndominium. Here are a few design options that can elevate your space:

- **Exposed Beams**: Nothing says barndominium quite like exposed wooden beams. They can frame your space by drawing the eye upward, adding a sense of grandeur and openness. Beams can be left natural for a rustic look or painted to match the ceiling for a more cohesive design.

- **Vaulted Ceilings**: By opening up the roofline inside, vaulted ceilings create an airy, expansive feel. They're especially effective in main living areas, where the added volume can make the space feel more luxurious and inviting.
- **Coffered Ceilings**: For a more structured and elegant look, coffered ceilings add depth through recessed panels. This design element is particularly effective in adding character to larger rooms or enhancing the formal feel of dining areas.

Choosing the right ceiling design can transform your barndominium from a simple structure into a breathtaking space that captivates and comforts all who enter.

Finish Selection Strategy

When it comes to selecting finishes for your barndominium, creating a cohesive look is key. Here's a strategy to ensure harmony across your space:

1. **Start with Inspiration**: Before making any decisions, gather images and samples of finishes that speak to you. This will help you define a cohesive aesthetic for your home.
2. **Consider the Flow of Space**: Think about how each room connects to the next. Choosing finishes that work together across different areas can create a sense of unity and flow throughout your home.

3. **Balance Texture and Color**: Mix and match different textures and colors to add depth and interest. For example, pairing smooth plaster walls with the roughness of exposed beams can create a dynamic interplay of textures.

4. **Test Your Choices**: Before committing, bring samples into the space to see how they look at different times of day and under various lighting conditions. This can help you avoid surprises and ensure you're happy with your selections.

Navigating the finishes for your floors, walls, and ceilings with a thoughtful strategy ensures every element of your barndominium's interior design works in harmony, creating a backdrop that's both beautiful and uniquely yours.

Lighting Your Barndominium: Strategies for Natural and Artificial Light

Light plays a pivotal role in shaping the ambiance and functionality of your barndominium. It's not just about illuminating spaces; it's about crafting an atmosphere that elevates your daily living. The right blend of natural and artificial light can transform any area into a welcoming and productive environment. Here, we'll explore how to achieve that perfect balance, ensuring your home is both beautifully lit and energy-efficient.

Maximizing Natural Light

The sun is the best light source available, not only because it's free but also because it positively impacts your mood and health. To make the most of natural light in your barndominium, consider the following:

- **Strategic Window Placement**: Think about where the sun travels during the day and position your windows to capture as much light as possible. South-facing windows pull in consistent light throughout the year, while north-facing ones provide steady, natural illumination with minimal glare.
- **Reflective Surfaces**: Incorporate materials that reflect light deeper into your home. Glossy floors, shiny countertops, and mirrors can all bounce light around, making spaces feel larger and brighter.
- **Skylights and Solar Tubes**: Sometimes, traditional windows just won't fit into your design. That's where skylights and solar tubes come in handy, funneling daylight from the roof into the heart of your home.

Artificial Lighting Solutions

When the sun sets, or on those cloudy days, artificial lighting takes center stage. Here's how to ensure it complements natural light and enhances your home's feel:

- **Layered Lighting**: Use a mix of ambient, task, and accent lighting to add depth and functionality. Overhead lights provide general illumination, pendant lights or under-cabinet strips cater to specific tasks, and floor lamps or wall sconces highlight architectural features or artworks.
- **Statement Fixtures**: Lighting fixtures aren't just functional; they're also decorative elements. A bold chandelier or a series of sleek, modern pendants can serve as focal points, adding personality and style.
- **Dimmers and Controls**: Install dimmers and smart controls to adjust the lighting based on the time of day, activity, or mood. This flexibility can transform the

atmosphere of a room with just a touch or a voice command.

Energy-Efficient Lighting

Reducing your energy consumption is good for both the planet and your wallet. Here are some tips to light your barndominium efficiently:

- **LED Fixtures**: Opt for LED bulbs and fixtures wherever possible. They use a fraction of the energy traditional bulbs do and last much longer, saving you money over time.
- **Smart Lighting Systems**: Automated systems can turn lights off when rooms are unoccupied or adjust the brightness based on the time of day, further reducing energy usage.
- **Natural Light First**: Design your daily activities and spaces around natural light, minimizing the need for artificial lighting during daylight hours. For instance, place reading nooks or workspaces near windows.

Lighting Design Tips

Creating a lighting plan that's both practical and pleasing to the eye requires a thoughtful approach. Consider these design tips:

- **Start with Function**: Think about what you do in each space and how lighting can support those activities. A well-lit kitchen island is essential for meal prep, while softer, indirect lighting creates a relaxing ambiance in lounging areas.

- **Mix and Match**: Don't be afraid to combine different styles and types of light fixtures. This eclectic approach can add visual interest and layers to your lighting design.
- **Consider Color Temperature**: The color temperature of light bulbs can dramatically affect the feel of a room. Warmer tones are comforting and ideal for living spaces, while cooler tones promote focus and are great for offices or workshops.
- **Highlight Architectural Features**: Use lighting to draw attention to architectural details like high ceilings, beams, or art niches. This not only adds drama but also showcases the unique aspects of your barndominium.

Crafting a well-lit home involves balancing the bounty of natural light with the necessity of artificial illumination. By strategically placing windows, choosing the right fixtures, and embracing energy-efficient solutions, you can create a space that's both functional and enchanting. Remember, lighting is not just about seeing better; it's about creating an environment that enhances your home's design and your quality of life.

Furnishing Your Barndominium: Blending Comfort with Style

Selecting furniture for your barndominium is like curating pieces for a personal gallery, where each item not only needs to look good but also has to fulfill a purpose. This is where you get to pair the practicality of everyday living with the look and feel that makes your heart sing. Here's how to strike that perfect chord between comfort and style in your furniture choices, ensuring every piece adds to the symphony of your home's design.

Furniture Selection

Choosing furniture that resonates with the scale and style of your barndominium ensures harmony within your living space. Large, open areas can handle oversized couches and tables without feeling cluttered, but smaller spaces benefit from sleeker, more compact pieces. When eyeing potential additions:

- Consider the lifespan and versatility of each piece. Opt for furniture that will age gracefully and adapt to evolving styles and needs.
- Test for comfort. It's not just about how a piece looks but also how it feels. After all, this is where life happens—from daily lounging to entertaining guests.

Space Planning for Furniture

Good space planning ensures that furniture arrangements enhance flow and meet the needs of your household without sacrificing style. Start by:

- Defining focal points in each room, whether it's a fireplace, a stunning view, or an art piece, arrange furniture in a way that complements these features.
- Leaving enough space for movement. A good rule of thumb is to allow at least three feet of walking space around furniture groupings.
- Using rugs to anchor furniture settings creates distinct zones within larger open spaces without the need for walls.

Mixing Styles

Your barndominium is a reflection of you, and mixing furniture styles is a wonderful way to express your unique taste. When blending different styles:

- Find a common thread that ties the pieces together, such as color, material, or design era. This creates a sense of cohesion amid diversity.
- Balance is key. Pair a hefty, rustic wood table with sleek, modern chairs for a look that's both grounded and airy.
- Remember, it's all about what feels right to you. Trust your instincts; if you love it, there's a place for it in your home.

Sustainable and Unique Finds

Incorporating sustainable furniture and unique finds not only adds character but also reduces your environmental footprint, making your barndominium as kind to the planet as it is stylish. To achieve this:

- Look for pieces made from sustainable or recycled materials. Many designers now focus on creating beautiful, eco-friendly furniture that tells a story of sustainability.
- Explore antique stores, flea markets, and artisan shops. These places are gold mines when it comes to finding unique items that bring a sense of history and craftsmanship into your home.
- Consider the backstory. Furniture with a history or made by local artisans adds layers of meaning to your space, making it truly one of a kind.

In wrapping up, remember that furnishing your barndominium is an adventure in itself. It's about finding the right balance between form and function, blending styles to create a look that's all your own, and making choices that reflect not just your personal aesthetics but also a commitment to sustainability. Each piece of furniture is a building block in the larger structure of your home, contributing to a living space that's both comfortable and visually engaging.

As we close this chapter, it's clear that the journey to creating a barndominium that mirrors your vision involves thoughtful consideration at every turn—from the broad strokes of design to the finer details of choosing finishes and lighting. Next, we'll explore the art of bringing life to these spaces through color, texture, and personal touches, ensuring your barndominium isn't just seen but felt, experienced, and loved.

FIVE

Laying the Groundwork - The First Step To Your Barndominium

igging your first shovel into the ground where your barndominium will stand is exhilarating and is like hitting the first note in a symphony—it sets the tone for everything that follows. But before that note resonates, there's a lot of tuning to be done. It's about getting the soil right, making sure the land sings in harmony with your plans, and ensuring every measure of the construction process is orchestrated perfectly. This chapter focuses on breaking ground, both literally and metaphorically. It's where your dream starts taking physical shape, rooted firmly in the ground upon which it stands.

Breaking Ground: Preparing Your Site for Construction

Site Assessment and Preparation

- Before any construction vehicle rolls in, a thorough site assessment is crucial. You're not just looking for a flat piece of land. You're checking for potential obstacles that could throw a wrench in your build—like rock formations that are tough to dig through or water tables lurking just beneath the surface, ready to flood your basement.

- **Clearing the Land**: This first step often involves removing any existing structures, trees, and other vegetation. It's a clean slate you're after, but remember, it's not just about bulldozing. Consider salvaging materials, donating usable fixtures, or repurposing trees as lumber for your project.

- **Grading and Leveling**: Once cleared, the land needs to be graded. This means creating a slight slope away from your building site to prevent water from pooling around your home. It's all about directing water away, keeping your foundation dry, and your future self happy.

- **Soil Testing**: Don't skip this. A soil test tells you about the ground's ability to support your structure. Some soils are too soft and need stabilizing, while others might require special foundation types. It's like getting to know the character of your land deeply before asking it to support your dream home.

Choosing the Right Foundation Type

The foundation is more than just the bottom layer of your home; it's what keeps your barndominium standing tall through storms and seasons. Selecting the right type is crucial and depends on several factors:

- **Soil Type**: Sandy soils drain well but might shift, requiring deeper footings. Clay soils, on the other hand, can expand and contract with moisture levels, demanding a more resilient foundation system.

- **Climate**: Areas with heavy frost require foundations that go below the frost line to prevent shifting during freeze-thaw cycles.
- **Barndominium Design**: Larger, multi-story structures need more robust foundations compared to single-story layouts.

Permits and Regulations

Getting your permits in order is like securing a backstage pass—it grants you the right to kickstart your project. Navigate this step by:

- **Understanding Local Codes**: Building codes vary widely by location. They dictate everything, from the depth of your foundation to the materials you can use.
- **Application Process**: Submit detailed plans of your barndominium, including the foundation design, to your local building department. Expect to pay a fee, and be prepared for a bit of a wait—they'll review your plans to ensure they meet all local codes and regulations.

Timeline, Budget, and Site Access Considerations

The foundation phase is both a significant time and money investment in your barndominium project. Here's how to manage both:

- **Timeline**: The foundation can take anywhere from a few weeks to a couple of months. Weather plays a big role here, as rainy days can delay pouring concrete or other critical steps.
- **Site Access**: You will need to ensure work crews can access the site with their equipment, delivery vehicles can easily

negotiate the terrain, and there is somewhere to drop and store materials. This applies to the entire project.

- **Budget**: This phase can consume a sizable chunk of your budget, especially if unexpected issues arise, like hitting bedrock when you least expect it. Having a contingency fund is crucial. Think of it as a financial cushion that helps you sleep better at night, knowing you're covered for those just-in-case scenarios.

In wrapping up, remember that laying the groundwork for your barndominium goes beyond just breaking the soil. It's about setting a solid foundation (literally) for the rest of your build. It's ensuring that the land beneath your feet is as ready for this adventure as you are, equipped to support not just the weight of a structure but also the weight of your dreams and aspirations. With the right preparation, permits, and plans in place, you're not just starting construction; you're crafting the very foundation of your future.

Foundation Types for Barndominiums: Choosing the Right One

Picking a foundation for your barndominium is a bit like selecting the right pair of shoes for a marathon. It needs to be sturdy, comfortable, and suitable for the terrain. Each foundation type has its own set of perks and quirks tailored to different needs and environments. Here, we explore the varied landscapes of foundation options, from the solid stance of slab-on-grade to the elevated perspective of pier and beam systems.

Slab-on-Grade Foundations

Imagine pouring a thick pancake of concrete directly onto the ground—that's essentially what a slab-on-grade foundation is. It's straightforward and robust, making it a popular choice for many barndominium owners. Here's a closer look:

- **Construction Process**: The process involves laying a concrete slab, usually about four to six inches thick, right on the prepared ground, reinforced with steel rods for extra toughness.
- **Benefits**: It's cost-effective and quick to install. Being directly on the ground, it offers excellent stability and is less prone to pest problems. It's also energy-efficient, as the concrete slab retains heat well.
- **Drawbacks**: The main downside is its inflexibility with plumbing and electrical systems, which need to be embedded in the concrete, making future changes or repairs challenging. Also, it can feel cold underfoot without in-floor heating.

Monolithic

- This foundation is comprised of a simultaneously poured slab and footings. The footings stabilize the slab, preventing movement due to soil shift, compression, or other external forces.
- **Structure**: Footings are deeper than the slab and resemble inverted Ts when viewed in section.
- **Benefits**: It is the preferred foundation type for barndominiums, offering a balance between affordability and structural integrity.
- **Engineering Considerations**: The design must adhere to local regulations, with footings extending below the frost line and proper use of rebar in both the slab and footings.

Stem Wall

The stem wall foundation is complex and costly, ranking above other types except for partial or full basements in barndominium construction.

- **Structure**: It involves pouring feet deep into the ground, followed by erecting a wall on top using poured concrete or cinderblock. A floating slab is then poured, complete with expansion joints adjacent to the stem walls.
- **Benefits**: The advantage here is that this foundation can be built with the wall high enough for a crawl space, allowing plumbing and other utility conduits to be accessed for maintenance or repair.

Engineering Considerations: This foundation is preferred for locations with substantial fill used for leveling, in areas with soil that expands and contracts, and for larger barndominiums.

Basement Foundations

Basements provide a whole additional level of living or storage space beneath your barndominium, making them a valuable addition to any home.

- **Added Value and Complexity**: Including a basement can significantly increase the square footage of your living space, offering room for everything from extra bedrooms and storage space to recreational areas. However, the excavation and construction process adds complexity and cost to the building project.
- **Design Considerations**: When planning a basement, think about its use early in the design phase. Natural light can be

maximized with well-placed windows or a walkout design
on sloping lots.
- **Waterproofing**: Keeping your basement dry is paramount.
Effective waterproofing strategies include exterior
waterproof membranes, proper drainage, and sump pumps
to manage any water that does accumulate.

Choosing the right foundation for your barndominium is a critical decision that affects not only the construction process but also the comfort, durability, and maintenance of your home in the long run. Whether you opt for the solidity of a slab-on-grade, the accessibility of a crawlspace, the added value of a basement, or the adaptability of alternative options like pier and beam, ensuring your foundation is tailored to your site, budget, and lifestyle will set your barndominium project on solid ground.

Framing and Exterior Construction: Building the Shell

The moment the foundation solidifies, the air around your plot thickens with anticipation. It's time to give your barndominium its skeleton—a frame to support and shape its very essence. This phase is where dreams start to resemble reality, inching closer with every beam and panel in place.

Materials and Methods for Framing

In the world of framing, two champions often go head-to-head: wood and steel. Each brings its own set of advantages to the construction arena.

- **Wood Framing**: A classic choice that's as old as the
construction itself. Wood is versatile, easily sourced, and
lends itself to quick adjustments on-site. It's warmer

underfoot and in ambiance, aligning well with the barndominium's often rustic allure. However, wood can be susceptible to moisture, pests, and fire if not treated correctly.

- **Steel Framing**: Enter the modern contender. Steel framing boasts incredible strength, doesn't warp or twist, and is impervious to pests and rot. It's also recyclable, making it a friendlier option for the planet. The downside? Installation requires specialized tools and skills, potentially driving up labor costs.

The choice between wood and steel often comes down to personal preference, budget, and the specific demands of your site and climate.

Exterior Wall Construction

Once the frame stands tall, wrapping it up to shield against the elements is next on the agenda. The construction of exterior walls is a multi-layered process, pivotal for both energy efficiency and structural integrity.

- **Sheathing**: This is the first layer applied to the frame, lending rigidity to the structure and providing a base for the siding. Plywood or oriented strand board (OSB) are common choices, each offering a good balance between cost and performance. Structural insulated panels (SIP) are an alternative, they are easier to install and are airtight, thus providing better insulation. This makes them a great choice for creating an energy efficient home.
- **Insulation**: Nestled within the wall cavity, insulation is the silent hero of energy efficiency. Fiberglass batts are widely used for their ease of installation and cost-effectiveness.

Spray foam insulation, while pricier, offers superior coverage and air-sealing capabilities.

- **Weather-Resistant Barriers (WRB)**: This layer protects against moisture infiltration, a critical step to prevent mold and water damage. House wraps or felt paper is typically used, enveloping the home in a breathable yet water-resistant shield.
- **Exterior Finish**: The final coat can be anything from traditional siding, brick or rock veneer, stucco, or even modern metal panels. Each option offers a distinct look and varying levels of maintenance, durability, and insulation.

Roofing Considerations

The roof, a barndominium's crowning glory, demands careful planning and execution. It safeguards your home from the elements while significantly impacting its appearance and appeal.

- **Material Selection**: Metal roofing, with its durability and ease of installation, is a favorite for barndominiums. Asphalt shingles, though more common in traditional homes, offer a vast color range and a softer look.
- **Ventilation and Insulation**: Proper attic ventilation prevents heat and moisture buildup, extending the life of your roof. Paired with adequate insulation, it ensures your home remains cool in summer and warm in winter, cutting down on energy costs.
- **Installation Steps**: Installing a roof is a stepwise dance, starting with a waterproof underlayment, followed by the chosen roofing material. Precision in overlapping and securing each piece is key to a leak-free, enduring roof and is definitely best left to the professionals.

Windows and Doors Installation

Windows and doors are more than just passageways and view-points; they are vital components in defining a home's character and comfort.

- **Energy Efficiency**: Look for windows and doors with high-performance ratings. Dual or triple-pane windows filled with inert gas and coated with low-emissivity (Low-E) films greatly reduce heat transfer, keeping your interiors comfortable year-round.
- **Security and Aesthetics**: Beyond energy considerations, the security features of windows and doors are paramount. Multi-point locking systems offer peace of mind. From a design viewpoint, the style, color, and material of your windows and doors should echo the overall theme of your barndominium, whether it leans toward sleek modernity or rustic charm.
- **Installation Guidelines**: Proper installation is crucial to the performance of windows and doors. Ensuring a tight seal all around prevents drafts and water infiltration. Employing flashing and correct sealing techniques guards against leaks while aligning with aesthetic considerations ensures your barndominium looks as good from the outside as it feels on the inside.

As you navigate through the framing and exterior construction phase, every choice—from the framing material to the last shingle on the roof—brings you closer to realizing your barndominium dream. It's a testament to precision, decision-making, and the harmonious blend of functionality and style. This stage sets the tone for the rest of your build, a critical point where your barndominium starts to take shape, promising the emergence of a home that's as robust as it is beautiful, ready to welcome you with open doors and wide windows into a space crafted uniquely for you.

Roofing Options for Durability and Aesthetics

When it comes to topping off your barndominium, the roofing material you choose plays a starring role not only in your home's protection but also in its overall look and feel. With the plethora of options out there, it's like picking the perfect hat—a balance between style, functionality, and how well it complements your outfit or, in this case, your barndominium.

Picking the Perfect Material

- **Metal**: Imagine the sound of rain on a metal roof, a comforting reminder of your barndominium's sturdy shield against the elements. Metal roofing, known for its longevity and minimal upkeep, suits a range of styles, from modern minimalism to rustic charm. It reflects sunlight, keeping your home cooler and slashing energy bills during those sweltering summer months.
- **Asphalt Shingles**: A classic choice that offers versatility in color and texture, asphalt shingles can easily match your barndominium's aesthetic. They're wallet-friendly and do a commendable job of protecting your home from rain, wind, and snow. Over time, however, they may require more maintenance than their metal counterparts.
- **Clay Tiles**: For a touch of timeless elegance, clay tiles can transform your barndominium into a Mediterranean retreat or a hacienda-style haven. Beyond their beauty, clay tiles excel in durability, often outlasting the very structure they cover. They do, however, tip the scales in weight and

price, demanding a stronger support structure and a bigger budget.

- **Recycled Slate Tiles**: Reclaimed from historical buildings, these tiles carry a story in every uniquely weathered piece, adding character to your barndominium. The eco-friendly charm of recycled slate tiles is a testament to both sustainability and timeless beauty, their natural color palette ranging from muted grays to deep blues, integrating seamlessly into various architectural styles. Slate's resilience against the elements means it withstands rain, snow, and wind with ease, maintaining its elegant appearance for decades. While they may come with a higher upfront cost, their longevity and low maintenance requirements make recycled slate tiles a wise investment for those who value heritage and sustainability.

Complementing Your Barndominium's Style

The right roofing material can accentuate your barndominium's architectural style, adding that "je ne sais quoi" that pulls everything together.

- For a sleek, industrial look, a metal roof in a standing seam style offers clean lines and a modern edge.
- Asphalt shingles, with their vast array of colors and textures, can be tailored to suit anything from a traditional country barn to a contemporary abode.
- Clay tiles, with their rich hues and distinct shape, imbue a sense of warmth and character, making them perfect for those aiming for a rustic or Spanish-inspired vibe.
- Recycled slate tiles, with their authentic historic charm, seamlessly blend the past with the present and lend an

unmatched sense of permanence and time-honored beauty.

Weighing Durability against Maintenance

Every roofing material has its own set of strengths and weaknesses when it comes to standing up to Mother Nature and the passage of time.

- Metal roofs can last up to fifty years or more with minimal care, making them an excellent investment for long-term durability. Occasional checks for dents or scratches suffice for maintenance.
- Asphalt shingles, while initially more affordable, typically have a shorter lifespan, around twenty to thirty years. They may require replacements for individual shingles damaged by severe weather.
- Clay tiles boast impressive durability, often lasting more than a century. However, they can crack under heavy impact, so checking for and replacing damaged tiles is advisable.
- Recycled slate tiles, when well-maintained, can last more than a hundred years. The exact lifespan can vary depending on the quality of the slate, installation, and local weather conditions, but it's common for slate roofs to remain functional and beautiful for over a century, making them one of the longest-lasting roofing materials available.

Prioritizing Energy Efficiency and Sustainability

Selecting a roofing material also offers an opportunity to enhance your barndominium's energy efficiency and reduce its environmental footprint.

- Metal roofing shines in its ability to reflect solar heat, reducing cooling costs and improving energy efficiency. Its recyclability at the end of its life adds to its green credentials.
- Light-colored asphalt shingles can somewhat reflect sunlight, though they generally offer lower energy efficiency than metal. Opting for shingles made from recycled materials can improve their sustainability score.
- Clay tiles' natural composition and durability make them an environmentally friendly choice. Their thermal mass helps regulate indoor temperatures, keeping your home cooler in summer and warmer in winter.
- Recycled slate tiles excel in their natural ability to regulate indoor temperatures, contributing to energy efficiency in your barndominium. Their dense composition acts as a natural insulator, helping to keep interiors cool in summer and retaining warmth in winter. This inherent property, coupled with the sustainable aspect of reusing materials, reduces the environmental impact associated with new raw material extraction and processing.

Gutters and Cupolas

Gutters

Some metal roofing systems omit gutters and downspouts, allowing water to flow off the edges of steeply pitched roofs. In the absence of gutters, it's recommended to extend the roof at least two inches beyond the eave and rake edges. Many barndominium homes, however, are built with extended overhangs that incorporate soffits and are usually equipped with gutters soon after the roof installation. Downspouts are typically added following the application of exterior siding. These gutters are positioned along the edge of the eaves and should be angled to ensure a minimum incline of 1/8 inch per foot toward the downspout.

Cupolas

- Cupolas are small, dome-like structures that sit atop a larger building, such as a barn. They serve both aesthetic and functional purposes; they provide ventilation and often natural light to the building below. Architecturally, cupolas add a distinctive element, enhancing the building's overall appearance. They are typically installed during the final stages of construction, crowning the roof and completing the structure's profile. In addition to their practical uses, cupolas can also house weathervanes or other decorative elements, making them a versatile and attractive feature on many buildings.

In selecting the crown for your barndominium, you're not just choosing a hat to keep the rain off; you're selecting a statement piece that protects, enhances, and reflects the essence of your home. From the practicality and sleek appeal of metal to the classic versatility of asphalt shingles and the timeless elegance of clay or slate tiles, your choice of roofing material lays the final touch on your barndominium, marrying form and function in perfect harmony.

Windows and Doors: Balancing Light, Views, and Energy Efficiency

In the quest to breathe life into a barndominium, the choices of windows and doors stand out as pivotal decisions. These elements do more than fill openings in walls; they frame the world outside, invite natural light to dance across your rooms and play a critical role in insulating your space. Let's navigate the decisions that ensure your views are maximized, your design choices are on point, and your energy bills are kept at bay.

Selecting Windows for Light and Views

Selecting the right windows is akin to choosing the lenses through which you'll see the world. The goal is to capture as much natural light as possible while framing the most appealing views of your surroundings. Here's how to strike that balance:

- Large, floor-to-ceiling windows not only flood your space with light but also create a sense of continuity between the indoors and outdoors.
- Bay windows, with their angled panes, catch light from multiple directions, ensuring a well-lit room throughout the day.
- For rooms where privacy is a concern, consider transom windows. Placed high on the walls, they let in light without compromising your retreat.

Door Types and Materials

Doors, both interior and exterior, set the tone for each room's character and the overall flow of your home. From welcoming entryways to intimate interior passages, the right doors in the right materials make all the difference.

- Sliding doors are perfect for spaces where you want to save room or create a seamless transition to outdoor areas.
- French doors, with their classic appeal, offer a touch of elegance, allowing light to filter through while maintaining an easy passage.

- Barn doors slide along a track, adding a rustic or industrial charm to your interior while being practical for areas with limited swing space.

In terms of materials, solid wood doors bring warmth and durability but might require more upkeep. Fiberglass and steel doors, often used for exteriors, provide excellent insulation and security with minimal maintenance.

Energy-Efficient Glazing Options

The glazing on your windows and doors is what stands between you and the elements. Investing in energy-efficient glazing keeps your home comfortable, reducing the need for heating and cooling.

- Double or triple glazing traps air between layers of glass, creating an insulating barrier that keeps interiors temperate.
- Low-emissivity (Low-E) coatings reflect infrared light, keeping your home warmer in the winter and cooler in the summer. They also protect against UV rays, preventing your fabrics from fading.

Installation Best Practices

Proper installation is the linchpin that ensures your windows and doors perform as expected. Here are some best practices to ensure a snug fit:

- Flashing and sealing are nonnegotiable. These prevent water from infiltrating around the frames, keeping your home dry and mold-free.

- For windows, make sure they're plumb, level, and square in the opening. Even a slight misalignment can compromise their operation and efficiency.
- Use expanding foam insulation around doors and windows for an airtight seal. It fills any gaps, preventing drafts and energy loss.

In wrapping up, the choices you make for your barndominium's windows and doors touch on everything from aesthetics and comfort to energy efficiency and security. Opting for styles that flood your home with light, materials that stand the test of time, and glazing that cuts down on energy use not only enhances your living space but also aligns with a sustainable approach to building. Moreover, ensuring these critical components are correctly installed guarantees their performance for years to come, making your barndominium not just a place to live but a sanctuary that opens up to the beauty outside while keeping you snug and secure within.

As we move forward, let's carry with us the understanding that our choices in materials, designs, and installation practices lay the foundation for a home that's as beautiful as it is functional. A barndominium is more than a structure; it's a reflection of our values, a testament to our creativity, and a shelter for our dreams. With the groundwork laid and the frame in place, we're ready to delve into the nuances of interior finishes and fixtures, where personal touches turn a building into a home.

SIX

From Framework to Functionality – The Heartbeat of Your Barndominium

I magine your barndominium as a living, breathing entity. The framing and exterior gave it shape and structure, but now it's time to instill the heartbeat—the systems that make it a functional, comfortable haven. Plumbing, electrical, HVAC, and smart home technologies aren't just utilities; they're the veins and arteries, the nerve center of your home, ensuring the seamless operation of a well-oiled machine delivering comfort and convenience.

Designing Effective Plumbing Systems

Water is a source of life, and in your barndominium, the plumbing system ensures it flows where and when you need it, without fuss or muss. Here's a breakdown of how to set up a system that works seamlessly:

- **Start with a Plan**: Before any pipes are laid, sketch out where your bathrooms, kitchen, and laundry room will be. Aim to keep them aligned vertically if your home spans multiple floors to simplify the plumbing lines.

- **Consider Water Pressure**: Nobody likes a dribble when they're expecting a strong shower. If your water source can't guarantee pressure, think about adding a pump or choosing fixtures designed for low pressure.
- **Insulate Pipes**: This is crucial to prevent freezing in colder climates. It also minimizes the noise of water rushing to its destination.
- **Go for Quality**: Choose durable materials like copper or cross-linked polyethylene (PEX) for your pipes. PEX, for example, is flexible, reducing the need for fittings and can significantly cut down on installation time and costs.

Electrical System Planning

Electricity is the spark that lights up your barndominium, powers your gadgets, and keeps your home humming. Proper planning ensures that it does so safely and efficiently.

- **Circuit Layout**: Plan circuits logically, separating lighting and power outlets and considering the demands of high-use appliances. This prevents overloading and minimizes the risk of tripping breakers.
- **Lighting Design**: It's more than just deciding where to put lamps. Think about task lighting in work areas, ambient lighting for general illumination, and accent lighting to highlight architectural features or art.
- **Outlet Placement**: Have you ever had to stretch a cord uncomfortably to reach an outlet? Avoid that by placing outlets every six feet or so in living areas, and consider convenience for charging stations and appliances.
- **Outdoor Outlets**: Consider both accessibility and protection from the elements. Position them strategically for garden tools, holiday lighting, and outdoor

entertainment needs while ensuring they are weatherproof and safely located away from water sources to prevent electrical hazards.

- **Future-Proofing**: As you lay out your electrical system, leave room for expansion. Additional circuits for a workshop, outdoor kitchen, or potential home addition save you from having to retrofit later.

Heating, Ventilation, and Air Conditioning (HVAC)

Comfort in your barndominium hinges on hitting that sweet spot in temperature and air quality. The right HVAC system is key, and here's how to choose it:

- **Size It Right**: An oversized system cycles off and on too frequently, while an undersized one struggles to keep up. Both scenarios can hike up your energy bills and reduce comfort. A professional can help calculate the perfect size based on your home's square footage, layout, and climate zone.
- **Consider the Types**: From traditional furnaces and AC units to heat pumps and radiant floor heating, each has its pros and cons. Heat pumps, for instance, offer both heating and cooling in one energy-efficient package but might not cut it in extreme climates.
- **Ventilation Is Vital**: Good air quality keeps your home smelling fresh and reduces the risk of mold. Ensure your HVAC system includes proper ventilation, particularly in areas like bathrooms and kitchens where moisture and odors accumulate.

Integrating Smart Home Technologies

Smart home tech brings your barndominium into the future, offering control, efficiency, and security at your fingertips. Here are some smart moves:

- **Start with a Hub**: Many smart devices need a central hub to communicate. Picking one that's compatible with a wide range of products gives you flexibility as you expand your smart home system.
- **Thermostats**: A smart thermostat learns your schedule and adjusts the temperature accordingly, saving energy without sacrificing comfort.
- **Security**: Smart locks, cameras, and alarm systems offer peace of mind, with the bonus of checking in on your home from anywhere.
- **Lighting and Appliances**: Smart lighting systems allow you to control ambiance and save energy, while smart plugs can turn any appliance into a smart device, offering control and monitoring for energy use.

In weaving together these essential systems, you're not just building a barndominium; you're crafting a space that responds to your needs, adapts to your lifestyle, and respects the environment. From the rush of water through pipes to the hum of electricity and the whisper of air circulating through vents, each element plays its part in creating a home that's as comfortable to live in as it is beautiful to behold.

Insulation Techniques for Energy Efficiency

Wrapping your barndominium in the right insulation is like giving it the perfect winter coat; it needs to keep the warmth in and the cold out and be comfortable enough to live with every day. The world of insulation materials is vast, each with its own unique strengths and ideal applications. Let's explore how to select the best-suited armor for your home, ensuring it stands strong against the elements while maintaining a cozy interior.

Choosing the Right Insulation Material

- **Fiberglass**: Ubiquitous and cost-effective, fiberglass insulation comes in batts and rolls, making it easy to install between wall studs and ceiling joists. It's a go-to for quick insulation jobs, but its effectiveness can wane if not properly sealed, and it requires safety gear to install due to tiny glass particles.
- **Cellulose**: Made from recycled paper products, cellulose is an eco-friendly option that's blown into walls, attics, and hard-to-reach places. It offers superior air-sealing capabilities but can settle over time, potentially reducing its insulative properties unless properly maintained.
- **Spray Foam**: This powerhouse seals leaks and gaps with a vengeance, expanding to fill every nook and cranny. Its higher upfront cost is offset by its excellent thermal resistance and air-sealing qualities, making it a wise choice for challenging spaces or extreme climates.

Thermal Bridging and Air Sealing

- **Understanding Thermal Bridging**: Imagine if you grab a metal spoon that's been sitting in a pot of boiling water;

the heat travels up the spoon handle. That's thermal bridging, but in your home's frame, heat bypasses the insulation through more conductive materials like wood or steel studs, wasting energy. Breaking these bridges involves adding insulative sheathing outside the studs or using less conductive materials in the frame construction.

- **Mastering Air Sealing**: Sealing your home against air leaks is critical. It's about stopping the uncontrolled flow of air through gaps and leaks, which can account for a significant portion of a home's energy loss. Techniques include caulking and weatherstripping around windows and doors and using spray foam or rigid foam boards to seal larger gaps.

Soundproofing Considerations

- **Materials for Peace**: Insulation isn't just about temperature; it's also a key player in soundproofing. Dense materials like mass-loaded vinyl or sound-deadening drywall can be incorporated into walls and ceilings to muffle sounds between rooms or from outside. Carpets and thick underlays can reduce noise levels, making interiors quieter and more serene.

- **Strategic Placement**: For optimal sound reduction, focus on insulating interior walls around noisy areas like laundry rooms, bathrooms, and media rooms. Double-insulating shared walls between bedrooms can also significantly improve sound privacy.

Insulation and Ventilation Balance

- **Breathing Easy**: Insulating your barndominium is about trapping the right amount of air inside—not too much, not too little. Ensuring your home can breathe is crucial to preventing indoor air from becoming stale, reducing pollutants, and preventing moisture buildup that can lead to mold and mildew.

- **Strategies for Healthy Air**: Incorporate passive ventilation strategies like operable windows for cross-ventilation or mechanical systems like heat recovery ventilators (HRVs) or energy recovery ventilators (ERVs) that exchange indoor and outdoor air without losing heat or coolness. Balancing insulation with adequate ventilation ensures your home is not only energy-efficient but also a healthy living environment.

Choosing the appropriate insulation materials and techniques for your barndominium is a critical step toward creating a comfortable, energy-efficient, and sustainable home. From easy-to-install fiberglass to eco-conscious cellulose and the all-encompassing seal of spray foam, the right insulation wraps your home in a protective embrace. Pairing this with thoughtful consideration for thermal bridging, meticulous air sealing, effective soundproofing, and a balanced approach to ventilation transforms your barndominium into a haven of comfort and tranquility, regardless of what the weather outside might say.

Drywall, Painting, and Finishing Touches

Stepping into this phase of creating your barndominium feels a bit like adding the final strokes to a masterpiece. It's where walls transition from mere structures to canvases awaiting your personal touch. This stage is all about detail, precision, and the choices that infuse your space with character and life.

Drywall Installation and Finishing

Hanging drywall transforms your barndominium from a skeleton of beams and studs into a place that's starting to resemble a home. Here's a stepwise approach to getting it right:

- **Measuring and Cutting**: Begin by measuring the area where the drywall will go, marking your sheets, and then cutting them to size, using a utility knife for precision.
- **Hanging**: Start at the top corner of a wall and work your way down, attaching the drywall to the studs using drywall screws. Ensure that seams between sheets are as tight as possible.
- **Mudding**: Apply joint compound (mud) over screws and seams using a wide putty knife. This part is more art than science, requiring a smooth, even application.
- **Taping**: While the mud is still wet, place a strip of drywall tape over the seams, pressing it into the mud. Once dry, apply another layer of mud over the top, smoothing it out as you go.
- **Sanding**: After the mud dries, sand the seams and screw spots to create a smooth, flawless surface. This might be the most tedious step, but patience pays off in the quality of the finish.

Choosing Paint Colors and Finishes

Selecting the right paint can dramatically alter the mood and perception of space within your barndominium. Here are some tips to guide your choice:

- **Test Samples**: Before committing to a color, buy samples and paint small sections of the wall to see how they look at different times of the day. Lighting can significantly affect how a color appears.

- **Consider the Mood:** Warm colors can make a room feel cozy but smaller, while cool colors can create a sense of calm and make spaces appear larger.
- **Finish Matters**: High-gloss finishes are durable and easy to clean, making them ideal for high-traffic areas. Matte finishes, however, hide imperfections better but are more challenging to maintain.
- **Paint Quality**: While it may be tempting to opt for cheaper paint, investing in higher-quality options pays off in the long run. Premium paints often provide better coverage, requiring fewer coats to achieve a uniform finish, and they tend to be more durable, resisting fading and wear over time. This means less frequent repainting and sustained aesthetic appeal, making the initial higher cost worthwhile for both appearance and longevity.

Trim and Molding Installation

Adding trim and molding is like framing a picture; it gives definition and polish to your rooms. It can be a decorative element that adds elegance or a simple finish that brings cleanliness to a space.

- **Material Choice**: Wood trim offers a classic look and can be painted or stained to match your decor. MDF, an engineered wood product, is a more affordable option and is best painted. PVC or polyurethane trims are durable and moisture-resistant, making them ideal for bathrooms or kitchens.
- **Design Options**: From the simplicity of a quarter round to the drama of crown molding, the type of trim you choose should complement the style of your barndominium. Even

the most basic trim, when painted with a contrasting color, can pop and define a space beautifully.

- **Installation**: Measure twice, cut once is the golden rule. Use a miter saw for angled cuts, especially for corners. Nail the trim in place, countersink the nails (use a tool to gently tap the nail deeper into the wood, so the top of the nail is not sticking out but is instead slightly below the surface of the trim), and fill the holes with wood filler for a smooth finish.

Final Touches for Personalization

Now comes the truly fun part—adding those elements that make the space uniquely yours:

- **Hardware**: Think of cabinet pulls, doorknobs, and light switch covers as jewelry for your home. They're small details that can make a big impact. Mixing metals can add visual interest but keep the overall aesthetic cohesive.
- **Decorative Finishes**: Consider a feature wall with wallpaper, wood paneling, or a bold paint color. These can serve as focal points and conversation starters.
- **Lighting Fixtures**: Beyond their practical purpose, lighting fixtures can serve as art pieces. An antique chandelier or a contemporary sculptural piece can elevate a room from ordinary to extraordinary.
- **Textiles**: Curtains, rugs, and cushions bring texture, color, and warmth into a room. They're also easily changeable, allowing you to update your space with the seasons or as your tastes evolve.

Each step, from the sturdy underpinning of drywall to the final flourishes of paint, trim, and personalized touches, brings your barndominium closer to being a home. It's in these details that a building breathes life, reflecting those who dwell within its walls, capturing the essence of home in every stroke, nail, and choice made. As you move through this phase, remember that it's not just about filling a space but about creating an environment where life unfolds, memories are made, and comfort is king.

Installing Interior Features: Kitchens and Bathrooms

When it comes to transforming a barndominium from a mere structure into a vibrant, living home, few spaces play as pivotal a role as kitchens and bathrooms. These areas, buzzing with daily activity, require a blend of functionality and personal flair. Here, we'll navigate the intricacies of designing these essential spaces, selecting flooring that resonates with the rhythm of home life and planning lighting that casts each room in its best light.

Kitchen Design and Layout

Crafting a kitchen that's both a joy to cook in and a place for families to gather starts with smart design. The layout is the backbone, influencing everything from the flow of foot traffic to the ease of meal preparation.

- **The Work Triangle**: This time-tested principle involves placing the sink, refrigerator, and stove at three points of a triangle to minimize unnecessary steps. Whether you're a gourmet chef or a microwave maestro, this layout keeps everything within easy reach.
- **Island Insights**: A well-placed island can serve multiple roles—from prep station to dining area to social hub. Incorporate storage options underneath for a mix of functionality and form.

- **Cabinetry and Appliances**: Opt for cabinets that reach the ceiling to maximize storage space and reduce dust-gathering gaps. When selecting appliances, think about how you use the kitchen. Energy-efficient models save on bills and support a greener lifestyle.

Bathroom Essentials and Luxuries

Bathrooms, though primarily functional, offer a canvas for luxury and relaxation. Whether you're fitting out a compact powder room or an expansive master bath, the right features can elevate the experience.

- **Smart Storage**: Vanities with built-in storage keep countertops clutter-free. Recessed medicine cabinets and shower niches for toiletries combine elegance with efficiency.
- **Luxury Touches**: Consider a walk-in shower with multiple showerheads for a spa-like experience. Heated floors and towel racks add a cozy warmth, inviting you to linger a little longer on cold mornings.
- **Fixture Selection**: Water-efficient fixtures in stylish designs allow you to save on utility bills without compromising on design. Soft, LED lighting around mirrors ensures the best light for grooming without harsh shadows.

Flooring Options

The right flooring marries style with durability, setting the tone for these hard-working rooms while standing up to the rigors of daily life.

- **Hardwood**: Its warmth and natural beauty make hardwood a favorite for living areas and bedrooms. Modern treatments and finishes now offer improved resistance to moisture, making it a viable option.
- **Tile**: Ideal for kitchens, bathrooms, and entryways, tile stands up to water and wear. Porcelain tiles, in particular, offer a blend of durability and design flexibility, mimicking everything from wood to marble.

Lighting Design for Ambiance and Functionality

Lighting does more than just illuminate spaces; it sets the mood, highlights design elements, and enhances functionality. A layered approach ensures that each room is lit to its full potential.

- **Task Lighting**: Under-cabinet lights in the kitchen or vanity lights in the bathroom provide focused illumination for precision tasks, reducing eye strain and improving safety. Consider motion activated for added eco-friendliness.
- **Ambient Lighting**: Soft overhead lights create a welcoming atmosphere in living areas and bedrooms. Dimmer switches or smart lighting allow you to adjust the ambiance to match the time of day or mood.
- **Accent Lighting**: Use directional lights to showcase artwork, architectural features, or special collections. It's a subtle way to add depth and interest to your spaces.

In outfitting your barndominium, every choice, from the functional layout of your kitchen to the luxurious touches in your bathroom, plays a role in crafting a home that's uniquely yours. Flooring selections lay the groundwork for each room's character, while thoughtful lighting design ensures that every space shines, both literally and figuratively.

Exterior Finishing and Landscaping: Creating Curb Appeal

Dressing up the exterior of your barndominium is like putting on that final outfit for a grand event. It's not just about looking good; it's about resilience, making a statement, and setting the stage for what lies inside. From the choice of siding to the layout of the landscape, every element plays a role in welcoming you home.

Exterior Finishes for Style and Protection

When it comes to choosing the right armament for your barndominium, think of siding, stucco, or brick not just as protective layers but as key players in your home's character.

- Siding options like vinyl or fiber cement offer a blend of durability and ease of maintenance, with a spectrum of colors to match your style. Consider board and batten for a touch of rustic charm or horizontal lap siding for a classic look.
- Stucco lends a smooth, continuous appearance that can be tinted to any color, fitting seamlessly with both modern and traditional designs. Its durability and resistance to fire and pests make it a wise choice for those in warmer climates.
- Both brick and stone bring timeless appeal and unmatched longevity. Whether left natural for a

historical vibe or painted for a contemporary twist, in the case of brick, both stand up to the elements with grace.

Deck, Patio, and Outdoor Living Spaces

Expanding your living space outdoors creates a seamless flow that encourages relaxation and connection with nature and is one of the major attractions to barndominium life.

- Decks made from wood or composite materials provide a raised platform perfect for dining al fresco or stargazing on clear nights. Incorporate built-in seating for convenience, and add a pergola for shaded comfort.
- Patios offer ground-level retreats that blend effortlessly with the landscape. Paving stones or concrete can be stamped and colored to complement your home's exterior.
- Outdoor kitchens elevate the cooking experience, allowing you to prepare meals surrounded by fresh air. Equip yours with a grill, a prep station, and a mini-fridge for the ultimate in outdoor dining.

Landscaping for Beauty and Functionality

The right landscaping not only enhances curb appeal but also serves practical purposes, providing privacy and supporting your lifestyle.

- Native plants thrive with minimal intervention, attracting pollinators while saving on water and maintenance. Group plants with similar water needs to create zones, simplifying care.
- Trees and shrubs offer privacy, shade, and a habitat for

birds. Position them strategically to frame views or shield your home from harsh winds.

- Edible gardens bring the joy of homegrown produce to your doorstep. Integrate raised beds or container gardens into your landscape for a blend of beauty and bounty.
- Outdoor lighting extends the enjoyment of your outdoor spaces into the evening. Solar path lights add safety and ambiance without the need for wiring.

Driveways and Walkways

The paths that lead to and around your home are as much a part of the landscape as the plants and structures.

- Materials like concrete, asphalt, gravel, or pavers should be chosen not just for their looks but for their performance under local weather conditions and their ability to handle the load of vehicles or foot traffic.
- Design should consider both aesthetics and functionality. Curved walkways invite exploration, while straight paths offer simplicity and directness. For driveways, ensure ample space for maneuvering and parking without compromising the green spaces.
- Accessibility is key. Consider the needs of all household members and visitors, including those with mobility challenges, when designing entrances and paths. Gentle slopes and nonslip surfaces make for a welcoming approach for everyone.

In wrapping up, the exterior of your barndominium and the surrounding landscape is more than just a facade or backdrop. They're an integral part of your home's identity, mirroring your style, meeting your needs, and welcoming you into a space that's uniquely yours. From the resilience of your chosen finishes to the inviting allure of your outdoor living areas and the thoughtfulness of your landscaping and pathways, every choice contributes to a home that's not just seen but felt. As we move forward, these decisions form the foundation for a living space that's as functional as it is beautiful and ready to be filled with life and memories.

SEVEN

Special Features of Barndominiums

Imagine your barndominium as more than just a place to live—it's your personal canvas, a space where functionality meets creativity. Now, think about adding a workshop or garage. It's not merely about having a space to park cars or store tools; it's about crafting an area that supports your hobbies, passions, or even your DIY projects. This chapter peels back the layers on how to seamlessly integrate these spaces into your barndominium, ensuring they're not just add-ons but integral parts of your home.

Design Considerations for Workshops

Creating a workshop within your barndominium calls for a blend of practicality and inspiration. Here's a rundown on making it both functional and inviting:

- **Space Requirements**: First off, decide how much space you'll need. If woodworking is your thing, you'll need ample room for both stationary machines and enough clearance to handle large pieces of lumber. For automotive work, consider the space for a vehicle, including room to walk around it comfortably and the area for tools and parts.

- **Tool Storage Solutions**: Imagine having all your tools within arm's reach but out of the way. Pegboards, sliding cabinets, and drawers under workbenches can keep tools organized yet accessible. For power tools, consider utilizing vertical space with sturdy shelving or racks.
- **Ventilation Systems for Safety**: If you're painting, welding, or working with chemicals, proper ventilation isn't negotiable. Options range from simple exhaust fans to more sophisticated air filtration systems that capture airborne particles and fumes, ensuring you're not trading your passion for your well-being.

Garage Integration and Functionality

Incorporating a garage into your barndominium is about envisioning a multipurpose space that extends beyond parking.

- **Vehicle Storage**: Naturally, your garage should accommodate your vehicles, but also think about future needs. Will you be getting a larger car, or maybe you'll need space for a boat or an RV? Plan for now and later.
- **Workshop Space**: Many opt to combine their garage with a workshop area. Setting aside part of the garage for hobbies or repairs can save on construction costs and provide a convenient, centralized spot for hands-on activities.
- **Home Gym Potential**: Garages can also make excellent spaces for home gyms. The typically more extensive, open area allows for various workout equipment, from

treadmills to weight stations, without cramping your style or your living space.

Insulation and Climate Control

Ensuring your workshop or garage is comfortable year-round means focusing on insulation and climate control.

- **Insulation**: It's not just for living areas. Insulating walls and doors can keep your workshop or garage comfortable, protect stored items from extreme temperatures, and even reduce noise.
- **Climate Control**: Options here include everything from simple space heaters or ceiling fans for a quick warm-up or cool-down to mini-split systems for more consistent temperature control. If you're spending a lot of time in this space, comfort is key.

Electrical and Lighting Needs

A well-designed workshop or garage shines, quite literally, with the right electrical setup and lighting.

- **Adequate Power Supply**: Ensure you have enough outlets and that they're placed where you'll need them most. For workshops, consider dedicated circuits for high-power tools to avoid tripping breakers.
- **Bright, Task-Oriented Lighting**: Good lighting is crucial, especially for detailed work. Overhead LED shop lights provide broad, bright illumination, while adjustable task lighting can focus on specific areas without casting shadows.

Integrating a workshop or garage into your barndominium is more than just an add-on—it's about fostering a space where functionality, safety, and personal passions intersect. Whether you're a hobbyist seeking a dedicated spot for your projects, someone needing a practical area for car maintenance, or simply looking for an efficient way to store and protect your vehicles, these spaces offer a blend of utility and personal satisfaction. With the right planning and design, your workshop or garage can become a seamless extension of your barndominium, reflecting your lifestyle and supporting your pursuits.

Designing for Pets and Livestock: Practical Tips

Creating a space that's welcoming for both your two-legged and four-legged family members requires a bit of foresight. For those of us sharing our lives and homes with pets and possibly livestock, it's all about blending functionality with comfort. Here, we cover how to integrate pet-friendly features and livestock accommodations into your barndominium, focusing on ease, safety, and cleanliness.

Pet-Friendly Design Features

Our furry friends deserve a spot in our homes that caters to their comfort and needs without sacrificing style or convenience. Here are a few ways to achieve that:

- **Durable Flooring:** Opt for pet-proof flooring options like ceramic tile, stained concrete, or luxury vinyl planking. These materials stand up to claws and accidents, making cleanup a breeze.
- **Built-in Feeding Stations**: Consider incorporating a feeding station into your kitchen design. A drawer that

pulls out with integrated bowls for food and water can keep feeding areas tidy and prevent spills.

- **Pet Washing Areas**: A dedicated pet wash station, possibly in a mudroom or laundry area, can be a game-changer. Equip it with a spray nozzle, an easy-drain floor, and pet-friendly grooming supplies. It makes bath time less of a chore and keeps the mess contained.
- **Sleep and Play Zones**: Designate a cozy corner or nook as a sleep and play area for your pets. Incorporate comfy beds, climbing structures, or toy storage to keep their belongings organized and encourage them to use these spaces.

Accommodating Livestock

For those incorporating livestock into their barndominium lifestyle, creating a harmonious living situation requires some planning.

- **Barns or Stables**: Situate these structures conveniently close to your home for easy access. Ensure they're well-ventilated, insulated for weather extremes, and designed for the specific needs of your animals, whether horses, goats, or chickens.
- **Ease of Access**: Design pathways or corridors that make moving between the barndominium and livestock areas seamless. Consider the use of durable, nonslip surfaces that are easy to clean.
- **Safety and Comfort**: The well-being of your animals is paramount. Use nontoxic materials and ensure enclosures are secure and free from hazards. Proper bedding, adequate space for movement, and access to water and outdoor areas contribute to their overall health.

Outdoor Pet and Livestock Considerations

The great outdoors is a playground for pets and livestock, but it also poses risks if not properly managed.

- **Fencing Options**: Secure fencing is crucial for keeping animals safe on your property. Options vary from traditional wood fences to electric livestock fencing. The choice depends on the type of animals and the level of security required, and detailed research is needed to ensure the correct type is utilized. (Word to the wise: goats think fencing is just a suggestion—but that's for a different book!)
- **Outdoor Shelters**: Provide shelters or shaded areas where animals can retreat from the sun or inclement weather. These can range from simple lean-tos for livestock to covered patios for pets.
- **Play and Grazing Areas**: Dedicate spaces for play and grazing that meet the needs of your animals. For pets, consider agility equipment or safe, enclosed areas to roam. Livestock will benefit from well-maintained pastures that offer ample grazing.

Maintenance and Cleaning Solutions

Keeping spaces used by pets and livestock clean not only ensures a hygienic environment but also contributes to the health and well-being of your animals.

- **Easy-to-Clean Surfaces**: Choose materials that are simple to clean and maintain for floors, walls, and any surfaces pets or livestock may come into contact with. Nonporous surfaces for indoor areas and durable, weather-resistant materials for outdoor spaces work best.

- **Storage for Supplies**: Implement storage solutions for pet and livestock supplies that keep items organized and accessible. Shelving, cabinets, or even dedicated storage rooms can house feed, grooming tools, and health care items neatly. Also, ensuring the storage area is not accessible to the livestock is key.
- **Waste Management**: Plan for efficient waste management, whether it's installing pet waste stations around your property or designing a manure composting system for livestock. Proper disposal or treatment of waste keeps your property clean and reduces the risk of disease.

In weaving these elements into your barndominium, you create a living space that's as inviting and comfortable for your pets and livestock as it is for the human inhabitants. It's about considering the needs and well-being of all your family members, ensuring everyone has a place to thrive. Through thoughtful design and intentional choices, your barndominium can become a haven that fosters health, happiness, and harmony for all.

Smart Home Technologies for Barndominiums

In the heart of every barndominium beats the pulse of innovation, where smart home technologies turn living spaces into realms of efficiency, safety, and pure enjoyment. These systems, once considered futuristic, are now within our grasp, offering a level of convenience and control that was hard to imagine just a decade ago.

Integrating Smart Home Systems

Incorporating smart home technologies into your barndominium brings a world of comfort and efficiency at your fingertips. It starts with a simple voice command or a tap on your smartphone, and suddenly, your living environment adjusts to your preferences. Here's how:

- **Automated Lighting**: Imagine lights that turn on as you enter a room or dim when it's time to relax. Smart lighting systems offer this convenience, along with the ability to change hues to match your mood or the time of day.
- **Climate Control:** Smart thermostats learn your schedule and preferences, adjusting the temperature to ensure comfort while optimizing energy use. On a chilly evening, your home can welcome you with warmth without running the heater all day.
- **Security Systems**: From cameras that allow you to monitor your property remotely to smart locks that can be controlled via your phone, integrated security systems offer peace of mind, knowing your barndominium is safe whether you're home or away.

Energy Management Solutions

Optimizing energy usage not only benefits the environment but also reduces utility bills, making smart home solutions an intelligent choice for the eco-conscious dweller.

- **Programmable Thermostats**: These devices go beyond simple temperature control, allowing for detailed scheduling and even learning your habits over time to adjust settings for maximum efficiency.

- **Solar Panel Monitoring**: For those harnessing the power of the sun, smart monitoring systems track energy production and consumption in real time, ensuring you get the most out of your solar investment.
- **Smart Appliances, Plugs, and Outlets:** Control appliances remotely, set schedules for operation, and monitor energy usage down to the device level, providing insights into where you can save.

Home Entertainment and Connectivity

The modern barndominium is a hub of digital connectivity, where entertainment and information flow seamlessly through living spaces.

- **High-Speed Internet**: A robust Wi-Fi network is the backbone of any smart home, ensuring smooth streaming, gaming, and browsing experiences throughout the house.
- **Smart Entertainment Systems**: From multi-room audio systems that sync with your playlists to smart TVs that access your favorite streaming services, the options for customized entertainment are endless.
- **Voice-Assisted Control**: Voice command devices can control not just media but also lighting, climate, and even order groceries, all without lifting a finger.

Future-Proofing with Technology

As technology evolves, so too should our homes. Ensuring your barndominium stays current requires a bit of foresight and planning.

- **Flexible Infrastructure**: When wiring your home, consider adding extra conduits and flexible pathways for cables. This foresight makes it easier to upgrade or add new technologies without major renovations.
- **Open Platform Systems**: Choose smart systems that work on open platforms, allowing for integration with a wide range of devices and the ability to add or upgrade components as new technologies emerge.
- **Education and Exploration**: Staying informed about the latest in smart home technology helps you make educated decisions about what features will best enhance your living experience. Regularly exploring new gadgets and systems can uncover opportunities to add convenience, efficiency, or fun to your barndominium life.

In weaving smart home technologies into the fabric of your barndominium, you're not just building a house; you're crafting a living experience that responds to your needs, adapts to your lifestyle, and embraces the future. From the whisper of automated shades drawing to a close at dusk to the gentle warmth of a climate-controlled room that welcomes you on a cold day, these technologies transform your barndominium into a sanctuary of comfort, convenience, and connection.

Creating Multipurpose Spaces: Offices, Studios, and More

In the heart of every barndominium lies a space that dances to the rhythm of multiple tunes. It's that corner where work meets creativity, where relaxation blends with productivity, and where guests find comfort in a space that's uniquely yours yet universally welcoming. This magic happens in multipurpose spaces—areas designed not just with a single purpose in mind but with the flexibility to adapt and evolve as your needs and desires change.

Designing Flexible Living Spaces

The secret sauce to crafting spaces that bend and flex without breaking lies in thoughtful design. It starts with envisioning how a room can serve you today and imagining what you might need tomorrow. A guest room doesn't have to stay a guest room if, for a few months a year, it doubles as your art studio. Likewise, an office space with a Murphy bed transforms into a welcoming room for visitors with just a flick of the wrist.

- Start with a clear layout that defines the room's primary function while leaving room for it to transform. Modular furniture and movable partitions can help delineate spaces without permanent changes.
- Choose a decor that complements multiple uses. Neutral walls provide a blank canvas for any activity, while accent pieces can add personality and define the space's current role.

Innovative Storage Solutions

Innovative storage solutions are your best friends for keeping these chameleon-like spaces functional and clutter-free. The goal is to have a place for everything, making transitions smooth and effortless.

- Fold-away desks and craft tables offer a workspace when you need one and disappear when you don't. Look for options that include built-in storage for tools and materials.
- Mobile storage units, like carts or trolleys, can be moved around or tucked away as necessary, making them perfect for art supplies, office gadgets, or even extra bedding.

- Convertible furniture, such as ottomans with storage inside or coffee tables that lift to become dining or work tables, is ideal for maintaining functionality without sacrificing space.

Incorporating Natural Light and Views

Never underestimate the power of natural light and scenic views in elevating a multipurpose space. Light has the power to energize and inspire, to calm and soothe, and to make any room feel more spacious and welcoming.

- Place desks and work areas near windows to take advantage of natural light and inspiring views. It boosts productivity and creativity, besides reducing the need for artificial lighting during the day.
- Use sheer window treatments, or consider installing skylights. They allow light to pour in while offering privacy, maintaining an open and airy feel even in compact spaces.
- For rooms with limited or no windows, consider the use of mirrors to bounce light around and create the illusion of space and depth.

Soundproofing for Privacy and Focus

In a home where walls wear many hats, keeping sound from traveling too freely is crucial. It ensures that a conference call in your home office doesn't turn into a household affair or that your late-night guitar practice doesn't disturb someone's sweet dreams.

- Start with the walls. Adding a layer of soundproofing drywall or mass-loaded vinyl can significantly reduce noise transmission. For existing walls, consider acoustic panels that double as art.

- Don't forget the floors and ceilings. Carpeting and rugs can muffle sounds, and adding insulation above ceiling tiles can prevent noise from traveling between floors.
- For doors, weather stripping isn't just for keeping out drafts. It also helps seal gaps through which sound travels. Solid-core doors block sound more effectively than their hollow-core counterparts.

In creating spaces within your barndominium that serve multiple purposes, you're not just optimizing square footage. You're building an environment that responds to the ebb and flow of life, one that offers sanctuary and stimulation, focus, and freedom, all within the same four walls. It's about making your home work for you, in every sense of the word, ensuring that every inch is living up to its fullest potential.

Outdoor Living Spaces: Decks, Patios, and Gardens

Turning your gaze outside, the transition from the cozy confines of your barndominium to the expansive embrace of nature should feel as seamless as stepping through an open door. This seamless transition isn't just about blurring the lines between inside and out; it's about crafting spaces that extend the warmth and personality of your home into the great outdoors. Whether you're sipping morning coffee on the deck, hosting a lively gathering on the patio, or losing yourself among the blooms of your garden, outdoor living spaces are the unsung heroes of a well-rounded barndominium.

Creating a Seamless Transition

Imagine stepping out from your living room onto a deck that feels like a natural extension of your indoor space. Achieving this level of seamlessness involves a few key strategies:

- Use similar or complementary materials for both indoor and outdoor flooring to visually connect the spaces. For instance, if you have wooden floors inside, consider a wooden deck or wood-look tiles for the patio.
- Large glass doors not only allow natural light to flood into your home but also offer unobstructed views of your outdoor haven, inviting the outside in.
- Consistent design elements and color schemes between your indoor and outdoor spaces ensure a cohesive look and feel, making the transition feel intentional and fluid.

Designing for Entertainment and Relaxation

Your outdoor spaces should cater to relaxation and entertainment with equal aplomb. Here's how to make sure they do:

- Outdoor kitchens equipped with all the essentials—grill, mini-fridge, and ample counter space—turn al fresco dining from an occasional treat into a way of life.
- Fire pits or outdoor fireplaces not only provide warmth and ambiance on chilly evenings but also become natural gathering spots for storytelling and laughter.
- Comfortable seating areas, whether through plush outdoor sofas or hammocks strung between trees, invite leisurely afternoons and long conversations under the stars.

Landscaping for Privacy and Beauty

While the openness of outdoor spaces is much of their appeal, a sense of privacy can make them feel more like a sanctuary. At the same time, the beauty of your landscaping contributes significantly to the overall atmosphere.

- Screening plants and hedges offer a living barrier that shields your outdoor living areas from prying eyes while adding a touch of greenery.
- Strategic placement of garden features such as fountains, sculptures, and flower beds draws the eye and adds layers of interest to your outdoor space.
- Incorporating a variety of plants with different blooming cycles ensures that your garden remains a riot of colors and textures throughout the seasons.

Embracing Sustainable Outdoor Practices

Sustainability should be as much a part of your outdoor spaces as it is of your indoor ones. Here are some ways to ensure your green thumb does more than just beautify:

- Drought-resistant landscaping reduces water usage while ensuring your garden stays vibrant, even in the heat of summer.
- Rainwater catchment systems, whether through barrels or a more integrated setup, allow you to water your garden and outdoor plants without tapping into the municipal supply.
- Organic gardening practices, from composting kitchen scraps to using natural pest deterrents, enrich the soil and

promote a healthier, more vibrant garden without the use of harmful chemicals.

In wrapping up, remember that your outdoor living spaces are not just add-ons to your barndominium but vital extensions of your home. They offer a bridge to the natural world, spaces where the air is fresher, the views more uplifting, and the connection to the earth more profound. By designing these areas with the same care and intentionality as you do your indoor spaces, you create a home that truly embraces all aspects of living, both inside and out. Now, as we turn our attention to the next chapter, we carry with us the understanding that a well-rounded home is one that offers sanctuary, connection, and a deep sense of belonging wherever we choose to rest our feet.

EIGHT

Overcoming Construction Hiccups – Navigating the Path Smoothly

Building a barndominium is a bit like baking a complex cake for the first time. You've got the recipe (your plans), your ingredients (materials and labor), and your oven preheated (land-ready). But just when you think you've got everything measured out perfectly, you realize your baking powder (budget) is off, or your oven's temperature (construction timeline) is not as reliable as you thought. Suddenly, that perfect cake (barndominium) you envisioned needs a bit more attention to get it just right. Here's how to tackle some of those common "baking" errors before they turn your dream build into a kitchen nightmare.

Underestimating Costs and Timelines

One of the biggest mistakes you can make is assuming everything will cost less and move faster than it realistically will. It's not pessimism; it's preparedness.

- **Real-Life Scenarios**: Picture this: You're halfway through construction when you discover the custom windows you ordered are on backorder for three more months. Or, the soil test comes back, and now you need a more expensive foundation. These aren't rare stories; they're almost par for the course.

- **Creating Accurate Projections**: Always add a buffer to both your budget and timeline. A good rule of thumb is to add 20% to your initial budget and a similar buffer for your timeline. This way, you're not caught off guard when (not if) surprises pop up.

Overlooking Local Regulations

Imagine painting your barndominium in a shade of vibrant turquoise, only to find out there's a homeowners' association rule against bold colors. It's crucial to know the rules of the game before you start playing.

- **Understanding Building Codes and Zoning Laws:** Check with your local building department and homeowners' association, if applicable, before finalizing your plans. Zoning laws can affect everything from your building's height to how close it can be to the property line. Ignoring these can lead to costly modifications or, in extreme cases, legal issues.

Choosing the Wrong Materials or Contractors

Picking materials and contractors is like selecting your baking team and ingredients. The quality of what goes into the project determines the quality of the final product.

- **Materials**: Opt for materials that suit your climate and lifestyle. For example, metal roofing might be pricier upfront but can save you on cooling costs in hot climates.
- **Contractors**: Don't just go with the lowest bid. Look for contractors with experience in building barndominiums. Ask for references and check them. A good contractor can mean the difference between a project that runs smoothly and one that's fraught with issues.

Neglecting Future Needs and Flexibility

Building a barndominium that suits your needs today but not tomorrow is like buying a pair of shoes that fit just right when you're standing still but pinch when you walk. Plan for flexibility.

- **Adaptable Spaces**: Design rooms that can evolve as your life does. An office might need to become a nursery, or a garage might need to become a workshop. Include plumbing and electrical capabilities in spaces that might change purpose, so you're not limited by infrastructure later.
- **Thinking Ahead**: Consider installing conduit for future electrical or internet upgrades. Planning for solar panels down the line? Make sure your roof can support them both structurally and in terms of orientation.

Visual Element: Checklist for Avoiding Common Mistakes

- Add at least a 20% buffer to your budget and timeline projections.
- Verify local building codes, zoning laws, and HOA rules before finalizing plans.

- Choose materials suitable for your climate and intended use.
- Select contractors based on experience, references, and a clear understanding of your vision.
- Design spaces with future flexibility in mind, considering potential changes in your lifestyle or family size.
- Plan infrastructure (plumbing, electrical) for easy adaptation to future needs.

Navigating the construction of your barndominium without falling into common pitfalls requires a mix of preparation, flexibility, and a good dose of realism. By understanding where others have stumbled, you can sidestep these issues and keep your project on a steady course. Remember, the goal isn't just to finish but to create a space that truly feels like home, both now and for years to come.

Handling Delays and Budget Overruns

Let's get real for a moment. If you're knee-deep in the construction of your barndominium, chances are you've encountered a delay or two. Maybe it's the weather throwing a wrench in your schedule, or perhaps it's an unexpected hurdle that has your budget doing the quick step. Whatever the cause, let's talk about strategies for dealing with these hiccups without losing your cool.

Anticipating and Planning for Delays

Delays are like uninvited dinner guests; they show up whether you want them to or not. The trick isn't to avoid them entirely (because, let's face it, that's nearly impossible) but to plan for their inevitable appearance. Here's how you can brace yourself:

- **Weather Wisdom**: Keep a close eye on the forecast. Certain seasons bring rain, snow, or even hurricanes. Schedule your most vulnerable tasks outside of these windows.
- **Permit Patience**: Permits can be slow to come by. Factor this into your timeline from the start. If you're ahead of schedule, consider it a bonus.
- **Material Buffer**: Supply chain issues? They're more common than you think. Order materials well in advance and have alternatives in mind should your first choice be delayed.

Managing Budget Overruns

Oh, the budget. That delicate balance between what you want and what your wallet can handle. When costs start to creep up, don't panic. Instead, take a deep breath and tackle it head-on with these tactics:

- **Priority Play**: List your project elements in order of importance. If the budget gets tight, you'll know where you can cut back without sacrificing your vision.
- **Open Line to Contractors:** Keep the communication lines with your contractors wide open. They should alert you the moment they foresee an overrun, giving you time to adjust.
- **Reserve Fund**: Remember that buffer we talked about? It's not just for timing. Having a financial cushion can save you a lot of headaches when unexpected costs pop up.

Staying Flexible and Adaptable

If there's one mantra you should adopt during this process, it's "stay flexible." Rigidity is the enemy of progress when it comes to construction. Embrace the fluidity of the process with these approaches:

- **Creative Solutions**: When faced with a challenge, get creative. Can't find the flooring you want? Explore alternative materials that might even add a unique touch to your space.
- **Phase It Out**: Consider phasing your project. If the budget's tight, focus on making the structure livable. You can always come back and add those luxurious finishes later.
- **Adapt Plans as Needed**: Sometimes, what looks great on paper doesn't pan out in reality. Be ready to tweak your plans. Often, it's these adjustments that lead to a better end result.

Learning from Setbacks

Every setback is a lesson in disguise if you're willing to look for it. Instead of viewing delays and budget overruns as failures, see them as opportunities to refine your plans and decisions. Here are a few ways to turn these situations to your advantage:

- **Feedback Loop**: After navigating a delay or budget issue, take a moment to reflect. What caused it? How was it resolved? This feedback can be invaluable for avoiding similar issues moving forward.

- **Vendor Vetting**: Ran into trouble with a contractor or supplier? Use this experience to refine how you vet and select your team in the future.
- **Budget Breakdown**: If you went over budget, break down the reasons why. This insight can help you plan more accurately next time, whether it's for an addition to your barndominium or an entirely new project.

Handling the twists and turns of barndominium construction with grace comes down to preparation, flexibility, and a willingness to learn from each bump in the road. With the right mindset and strategies, you can navigate through delays and budget overruns, keeping your project on track toward creating the home of your dreams.

Maintaining Good Communication with Your Building Team

Communication, in the grand scheme of constructing a barndominium, is like the oil in an engine—it keeps everything running smoothly and prevents the gears from grinding to a halt. Establishing a rapport with your building team, setting clear expectations, and navigating the inevitable disagreements are all crucial steps in ensuring your project doesn't just survive but thrives from foundation to finish.

Establishing Clear Communication Channels

In the early days, when the excitement is palpable and the ground is yet to be broken, setting up clear lines of communication with your team can seem like a formality. Yet, it's anything but. Here's a look at how to keep everyone on the same page:

- **Regular Meetings**: Schedule them like clockwork, whether weekly or biweekly, to set expectations, review progress, discuss upcoming tasks, and address any concerns. This regularity keeps everyone aligned and accountable.
- **Digital Tools**: Utilize project management apps or group chats to share updates, documents, and quick messages. It's the equivalent of having a virtual meeting room accessible to everyone involved at any time.
- **Point of Contact**: Designate a primary point of contact on both ends. This streamlines communication, ensuring messages aren't lost in translation across multiple channels.

Setting Expectations and Roles

As the project kicks off, it's tempting to assume everyone shares your vision and understands their role in bringing it to life. However, assumptions can lead to misunderstandings. Here's how to set the stage right:

- **Clear Roles**: Define who is responsible for what, from the architect drawing up the plans to the contractor overseeing the daily build. Knowing who to turn to for specific issues prevents confusion.
- **Project Goals**: Share your vision and objectives with the team. It's not just about building a structure; it's about creating a home that meets specific needs and desires.
- **Feedback Loop**: Encourage open feedback from the get-go. It fosters a culture of transparency and continuous improvement, which is essential for navigating the project's ups and downs.

Navigating Disagreements or Misunderstandings

Even with the best-laid plans, disagreements or misunderstandings will arise. It's natural when multiple minds and skill sets converge on a complex project. Here's how to steer through these choppy waters:

- **Listen First**: When a disagreement arises, listen to understand, not to respond. Often, conflicts stem from miscommunications that can be easily resolved once all perspectives are heard.
- **Solution-Oriented Approach**: Focus on finding a solution rather than dwelling on the problem. Brainstorming together can turn a disagreement into a stepping stone toward a better outcome.
- **Mediation**: If a resolution seems out of reach, don't hesitate to bring in a neutral third party to mediate. Sometimes, an external perspective is what it takes to bridge the gap.

Building a Collaborative Relationship

The relationship with your building team shouldn't just be transactional; it should be collaborative. After all, you're working together to create something that stands long after the last nail is hammered. Here's how to cultivate this partnership:

- **Respect Expertise**: Recognize and respect the expertise each team member brings to the table. Their insights and suggestions can often save time, money, or future headaches.
- **Shared Success**: Celebrate milestones together. Completing a stage in the construction process is a

collective achievement, and recognizing it as such bolsters morale and team spirit.

- **Open Door Policy**: Encourage open communication, letting the team know that their ideas, concerns, and suggestions are always welcome. It's in these exchanges that innovative solutions and improvements are often found.

In essence, maintaining good communication with your building team is about more than just keeping everyone informed—it's about building trust, fostering collaboration, and steering the project through both calm and stormy seas with a steady hand. It's the recognition that, while the blueprint outlines the structure, it's the strength of the relationships and the clarity of communication that truly build a home.

Adapting to Changing Plans and Requirements

In the dance of constructing a barndominium, flexibility is your rhythm, and adaptation is your steps. The floor beneath you might shift—be it through changes in design, materials, or the ever-watchful eye of regulations. Keeping in step without missing a beat? That's the art we're mastering here.

Flexibility in Design and Construction

Imagine you're painting a masterpiece, but the hues on your palette change mid-stroke. In building, your materials, technology, and even personal tastes evolve. Here's how to stay fluid:

- **Modular Design**: Think of your barndominium as a collection of spaces that can change as your needs do. A

room might start as an office and evolve into a nursery or hobby room. Design with this evolution in mind.
- **Material Flexibility**: Sometimes, that perfect tile you picked out is suddenly out of stock. Having a Plan B (and even C) that still fits your vision ensures you don't hit pause while waiting for that one material.
- **Regulation Adaptation**: Building codes can be updated without warning. Staying in close contact with local building authorities and being ready to tweak your plans ensures you're always in compliance, avoiding costly re-dos.

Managing Scope Creep

Scope creep—when your project slowly becomes something much larger than initially planned—can be a silent budget and timeline buster. Keeping it in check requires vigilance.

- **Clear Objectives**: Before breaking ground, outline the must-haves and nice-to-haves of your project. This clarity helps when deciding whether to expand your scope or stick to the original plan.
- **Change Control Process**: Implement a process for reviewing and approving changes. Every addition should be evaluated for its impact on the budget and timeline, ensuring you make informed decisions.
- **Regular Reviews**: Hold regular check-ins with your team to assess progress and discuss any potential changes. These meetings are opportunities to realign objectives and make necessary adjustments.

Decision-Making under Pressure

When time is of the essence and a decision needs to be made, the pressure can cloud judgment. Here are strategies to ensure your decisions are sound, even when the clock is ticking:

- **Information Gathering**: Quick decisions still need to be informed decisions. Gather as much relevant information as possible in the time available, focusing on data that directly impacts the decision at hand.
- **Risk Assessment**: Weigh the potential outcomes. What's the worst that could happen with each option? Understanding the risks involved helps you make a choice that aligns with your project's long-term success.
- **Consult the Team**: Use the collective wisdom of your team. Different perspectives can shed light on aspects you might not have considered, leading to a more rounded decision.

Learning from the Process

Every twist and turn in the construction of your barndominium is rich with lessons. Embracing these as opportunities for growth transforms challenges into invaluable insights.

- **Reflective Practice**: After navigating a significant change or decision, take time to reflect. What led to this situation? How effective was your response? This reflection turns experience into wisdom.
- **Documenting Lessons**: Keep a project journal or log where you note challenges, solutions, and outcomes. This record becomes a treasure trove of insights for future projects or phases.

- **Sharing Knowledge**: Construction is a collective endeavor. Share what you learn with your team, and encourage them to do the same. This culture of learning elevates the entire project, making each step forward more informed than the last.

In crafting your barndominium, the ability to adapt to changing plans and requirements is not just a skill but a necessity. It ensures that your project remains resilient against the unexpected, turning potential setbacks into stepping stones toward creating a home that truly reflects your vision. Through flexible design, careful management of scope creep, decisive action under pressure, and a commitment to learning from the process, you pave a path through the complexities of construction. This journey, filled with adaptation and growth, leads not just to the completion of a structure but to the realization of a dream.

Final Inspections and Moving In: The Last Hurdle

Crossing the finish line of your barndominium build involves a few critical steps before you can truly call it home. From ensuring everything is up to code with final inspections to the actual moving-in process, let's walk through what you need to keep in mind.

Preparing for Final Inspections

The final inspection is not just a formality; it's a safeguard that ensures your barndominium meets all necessary building codes and safety standards. Getting ready for this step means:

- **Gathering Documentation**: Have all your permits, construction documents, and any change orders organized and ready for review. This paperwork is crucial for inspectors to verify that the work has been completed as planned.

- **Creating a Checklist**: Develop a pre-inspection checklist based on your initial building plan and any relevant local codes. This list should cover structural elements, electrical systems, plumbing, and any other areas subject to inspection.
- **Doing a Walk-Through**: Before the inspector arrives, do a thorough walk-through of your barndominium using your checklist. Fix any minor issues you might find, such as a leaky faucet or a missing handrail, to help the inspection go smoothly.

Addressing Inspection Findings

Even with meticulous planning, the inspector might find issues that need addressing. Here's how to handle those findings:

- **Understanding the Report**: First, make sure you fully understand the issues the inspector has pointed out. Ask questions if anything is unclear.
- **Prioritizing Fixes**: Some issues might be minor and easily fixed, while others could require more significant work. Prioritize based on safety and compliance.
- **Hiring Professionals**: For more complex fixes, it might be necessary to bring back your contractor or a specialist. Ensure they understand the inspection report and what's required to resolve the issues.

The Moving-In Process

Moving in can be both exciting and overwhelming. Here are some tips to make the transition smoother:

- **Planning the Move**: Start by deciding what will move with you and what might need to be stored or sold. If you're using a moving company, get quotes and schedule your move date well in advance.
- **Setting Up Utilities**: Ensure all your utilities are set up and functioning before moving day. This includes electricity, water, internet, and any other services you'll need from day one.
- **Personalizing Your Space**: Begin with the essentials, but also think about how you want to personalize your new space. Whether it's painting walls or hanging art, these touches quickly make a new house feel like home.

Post-Move Adjustments and Settling In

Once you're in, give yourself time to adjust and settle. This phase is about:

- **Unpacking Strategically**: Start with the necessities and gradually unpack the rest. This approach prevents clutter and allows you to think carefully about the placement of items.
- **Learning Your Home**: Spend the first few weeks getting to know your barndominium. Notice how light moves through the space, where you naturally prefer to spend your time, and how you use each room.
- **Making Adjustments**: As you live in your space, you might find that certain areas could function better with a

bit of tweaking. Be open to rearranging furniture or even undertaking minor projects to enhance functionality and comfort.

Transitioning from the construction phase to living in your barndominium is a period filled with anticipation and discovery. From ensuring everything meets the mark with final inspections to putting your personal stamp on the space, each step brings you closer to creating the home you've envisioned. It's a time of culmination, where planning, patience, and hard work pay off, allowing you to start making memories in a place truly your own.

As we wrap up this chapter, remember that the journey from the blueprint to the barndominium is paved with decisions, challenges, and achievements. The final inspection marks a significant milestone, not just in terms of construction but in realizing your vision. Moving in and settling into your new space is the beginning of a new chapter, filled with the promise of making your barndominium a backdrop for life's moments, big and small. Let's carry forward the lessons learned and the experiences gained as we continue to build not just homes but lives filled with meaning and joy.

NINE

Tailoring Spaces – Floor Plans for Every Lifestyle

P icture this: A blank canvas in front of you—not the kind artists splash paint on, but the architectural kind where dreams morph into floor plans. Here, the rules aren't dictated by tradition but by the rhythm of your life. This chapter isn't just about laying out rooms; it's about sculpting spaces that echo your heartbeat, whether it's the pitter-patter of little feet, the clinking of glasses in celebration, or the serene silence of a cozy nook.

Floor Plans for Every Lifestyle

Every lifestyle demands a unique spatial solution. Think of a musician needing a sound-proof studio or a large family where each member yearns for their own personal nook. The versatility of barndominiums shines here, offering a spectrum of floor plans tailored to diverse living needs. Let's explore how these plans can be adapted, highlighting efficiency, flow, adaptability, and those special features that make a house a home.

Diverse Living Needs

- **Single Dwellers**: Compact yet open floor plans that maximize every square inch, offering a blend of functionality and style. Think studio-style layouts with sleek, hidden storage solutions.
- **Large Families**: Emphasis on privacy and communal spaces. Bedrooms strategically placed for quietness, with ample living areas where everyone gathers.
- **Work-from-Home Professionals**: Office spaces with natural light, away from the household's hustle and bustle, yet close enough to stay connected.

Efficiency and Flow

- **The Heart of the Home**: Kitchens with islands that serve as the command center, opening up to living areas for an inclusive vibe.
- **Zoned Yet Open**: Separation of sleeping quarters from day areas, ensuring restful sanctuaries without sacrificing the open concept.

Adaptability and Future-Proofing

- **Growing with You**: Rooms designed with flexibility in mind. A nursery that transforms into a study or a hobby room that becomes a guest suite.
- **Outdoor Connection**: Plans that extend living spaces outdoors, with patios or decks seamlessly integrated, blurring the lines between inside and out.

Highlighting Unique Features

- **Ceiling Heights**: Playing with ceiling heights to define areas within an open floor plan, adding character and spatial interest.
- **Multipurpose Rooms**: Rooms equipped with fold-away furniture or built-ins, ready to change function based on current needs—from a home gym to a playroom in a snap.

These samples are a starting point and a source of inspiration. Remember, the best floor plan for you is one that reflects your lifestyle, anticipates your future, and brings joy with every step you take within your barndominium.

Checklist for Choosing Your Floor Plan

- **Location of Bedrooms**: Consider morning and evening routines, ensuring minimal disturbance.
- **Kitchen Layout**: Think about your cooking habits. Do you entertain often? Is a large pantry a must-have?
- **Work and Play**: Ensure there's a dedicated space for work or hobbies that require concentration, away from the main living areas.
- **Outdoor Access**: Easy access to outdoor spaces can change how you live. Imagine breakfasts on the deck or evening gatherings around a fire pit.

This checklist is a tool to ensure the floor plan you settle on aligns with your day-to-day life, making your barndominium not just a place to live but a place that enhances how you live.

As we dissect these floor plan samples, it's clear that each square foot has a purpose, and each design choice reflects a need or desire. The beauty of building a barndominium lies in this very flexibility—the power to tailor not just the aesthetics but the very layout of your home to match the rhythm of your life. Whether you're a bustling family in need of space and synergy, a remote worker seeking solitude without isolation, or simply someone craving a home that breaks the mold, these floor plans serve as a canvas, ready to be painted with the colors of your unique lifestyle.

Gallery of Barndominium Interiors: From Rustic to Modern

Diving into the heart of barndominium design, we explore the vast sea of interior styles, from the warmth of rustic charm to the crisp lines of modern minimalism. This gallery isn't just a visual feast; it's a map for navigating the broad spectrum of design possibilities that barndominiums offer. Each style speaks a unique language, and understanding their elements can help you articulate your own interior design dreams.

Showcasing a Range of Styles

Barndominiums are unique in their ability to morph from the rugged aesthetics of a countryside barn to the sleek finishes of a downtown loft. Here, we'll walk through a series of interiors that capture this diversity:

- **Rustic Elegance**: Exposed wooden beams, distressed wood floors, and antique furniture pieces create a space that's both inviting and steeped in history.
- **Modern Minimalism**: Clean lines, a monochrome color palette, and uncluttered spaces define this style, where less is truly more.
- **Industrial Chic**: Think polished concrete floors, metal

fixtures, and a neutral color scheme accented by raw, unfinished textures.

- **Bohemian Bliss**: Vibrant colors, eclectic furniture, and an abundance of greenery characterize this free-spirited approach to interior design.

Detailing Elements of Design

Breaking down these styles further, we highlight the key elements that you can incorporate into your own barndominium:

- **Color Schemes**: Rustic interiors often embrace warm, earthy tones, while modern spaces might lean toward stark whites or grays. Bohemian designs, on the other hand, aren't afraid to play with a kaleidoscope of colors.
- **Materials and Finishes**: Wood is a staple in rustic designs, both in its natural form and distressed. Modern interiors might feature glass and steel with polished finishes. Industrial spaces often showcase materials in their raw, unfinished state.
- **Furniture and Decor**: Rustic designs might include chunky wooden furniture and handmade textiles. Minimalist spaces opt for sleek, functional pieces. In bohemian interiors, vintage finds and unique artifacts add personality and warmth.

Innovative Use of Space

In barndominiums, every square inch counts. Here are examples of interiors that maximize their footprint without sacrificing style:

- **Open Floor Plans**: Merging the kitchen, dining, and living areas not only creates an airy, expansive feel but also enhances social interaction.
- **Multi-Functional Rooms**: A home office by day can transform into a guest room at night thanks to Murphy beds and convertible furniture.
- **Smart Storage Solutions**: Built-in shelves, hidden cabinets, and multi-purpose furniture pieces keep clutter at bay and maintain the aesthetic appeal of the space.

Personal Touches That Make a Space

What transforms a house into a home are the personal touches that reflect the lives and loves of those who dwell within:

- **Family Heirlooms**: A weathered chest or an heirloom quilt can add depth and history to your space, creating a link to the past.
- **Art Collections**: Whether it's fine art, street art, or children's drawings, displaying art makes a statement about your personal taste and what inspires you.
- **DIY Projects**: Handcrafted decor, from macramé wall hangings to custom-built furniture, infuses your space with a sense of accomplishment and uniqueness.

Virtual Design Board

- Imagine a digital corkboard where you can pin ideas, color swatches, furniture pieces, and layout plans. This tool lets you mix and match elements until you find the perfect combination for your space.

Design Vocabulary Glossary

- A comprehensive glossary that demystifies design terminology, from "chiaroscuro" to "wabi-sabi." Understanding these terms not only makes you a more informed designer but also helps you communicate your vision more clearly.

In peeling back the layers of barndominium interior designs, we uncover not just the aesthetics but the functionality and personal expression that these spaces allow. Whether you lean toward the rustic charm that speaks of legacy and warmth, the clean lines of modern design that echo with simplicity and calm, the raw, textured appeal of industrial chic, or the vibrant, eclectic vibe of bohemian style, your barndominium is a canvas waiting for your brush. Through the thoughtful selection of color schemes, materials, and finishes, and by embracing innovative use of space and personal touches, you can craft interiors that are not only visually stunning but deeply personal.

Landscaping Ideas for Your Barndominium

Transforming the outdoor space around your barndominium into a harmonious extension of your home is not just about aesthetics; it's about creating an environment that complements your lifestyle and connects you to the natural world. With thoughtful landscaping, your outdoor area can become a sanctuary for relaxation, a hub for entertainment, or a private retreat, all while enhancing the beauty and functionality of your property.

Melding Home with Nature

The true essence of a barndominium blends industrial strength with rustic charm, and extending this balance into your outdoor space can yield stunning results. Here are ways to achieve that seamless integration:

- Use native stone and wood in outdoor structures like pergolas, benches, or paths to mirror the barndominium's materials, forging a natural connection between the building and its surroundings.
- Plan your garden layouts and plant selections to complement the lines and colors of your home. If your barndominium features warm wood tones, plantings with burgundy leaves or vibrant greens can accentuate this palette.
- Water features, such as ponds or waterfalls, can introduce a dynamic element to your landscape, drawing in wildlife and providing a tranquil auditory backdrop that enhances the sense of being close to nature.

Embracing Sustainability and Ease

In today's world, the choice to go green is both a lifestyle statement and a necessity. Here are ideas to create a landscape that respects the earth and simplifies your life:

- **Native Plantings**: Choose plants native to your area for your gardens. They're not only more likely to thrive with minimal intervention but also support local wildlife, such as pollinators and birds.
- **Xeriscaping**: This landscaping method focuses on water efficiency, using drought-resistant plants and innovative

irrigation techniques to reduce your water usage and maintenance needs.

- **Organic Gardening**: By avoiding chemical pesticides and fertilizers, you protect the ecosystem around your barndominium. Composting kitchen scraps and yard waste can provide nutrient-rich soil for your plants, closing the loop on waste.

Creating Spaces for Outdoor Living and Recreation

Your outdoor space should be an extension of your home's living areas, offering comfort and functionality. Here's how you can create inviting outdoor living areas:

- Designate zones for different activities, such as a dining area with a built-in grill for al fresco meals, a cozy fire pit seating area for evening gatherings, and a clear, flat lawn space for games and activities.
- Install lighting to extend the usability of your outdoor areas into the evening. Solar path lights, string lights, and strategically placed spotlights can create an enchanting atmosphere after sunset.
- For those who enjoy gardening, raised garden beds can be both an aesthetic feature and a practical way to grow herbs, vegetables, or flowers. They can be designed to complement the barndominium's architecture while also making gardening more accessible.

Enhancing Privacy and Security with Strategic Landscaping

While the open spaces around a barndominium are one of its charms, there are ways to create privacy and increase security without compromising the sense of openness.

- **Living Walls**: Tall hedges or climbing plants on trellises can form natural barriers that shield your outdoor living areas from view, providing privacy without the need for fences.
- **Strategic Tree Planting**: Trees can be planted to block sightlines from the road or neighboring properties, offering seclusion while also adding beauty and shade.
- **Natural Surveillance**: Keep garden paths clear and ensure there are no hidden areas where intruders could lurk. The principle of natural surveillance suggests that visibility increases security, so design your landscape to allow unobstructed views from the house to the far reaches of your property.

In crafting the landscape around your barndominium, consider how each element, from the choice of plants to the design of outdoor living spaces, contributes to a cohesive environment that reflects your lifestyle and values. Whether it's through the integration of home with nature, the adoption of sustainable practices, the creation of functional outdoor areas, or the enhancement of privacy and security, your landscaping choices have the power to transform your barndominium's surroundings into a vibrant, welcoming extension of your home.

Resources and Tools for the Aspiring Barndominium Builder

In the world of barndominium building, having the right set of tools and resources at your disposal can make all the difference. It's not just about the physical tools you use to construct your dream home but also about the wealth of knowledge, support, and inspiration you surround yourself with throughout the process. From the earliest stages of design to the final touches that make your space uniquely yours, here's a curated selection of resources and tools designed to assist you every step of the way.

Comprehensive Resource List

A well-assembled toolkit is your first step toward turning your barndominium vision into reality. This list includes a variety of resources, each serving a unique purpose in your building journey:

- **Books**: There are many books out there that offer practical advice and step-by-step instructions, covering everything from budgeting to the construction process.
- **Websites**: Platforms such as Houzz and ArchDaily provide endless inspiration, showcasing a wide range of architectural styles and interior designs while offering articles, guides, and case studies.
- **Forums**: Websites like Reddit's r/Homebuilding, r/barndominium, or the Barndominium Life Forum are invaluable for connecting with others on the same path, sharing experiences, asking questions, and receiving advice.
- **Software Tools**: For those looking to dive into the design aspect, software like SketchUp offers user-friendly interfaces for creating detailed plans and 3D models of your future home.

Design and Planning Tools

Visualizing your dream home and translating that vision into actionable plans is a crucial part of the building process. The below tools are specifically designed to help you refine your designs and bring them to life:

- **CAD Software**: Programs like AutoCAD and Revit allow for precise architectural planning and customization, giving you the power to tweak every detail of your design.
- **Online Floor Plan Creators**: Websites such as Floorplanner and RoomSketcher enable you to create and experiment with different layouts and designs without the need for advanced technical skills.
- **Virtual Reality Apps**: Apps like VR Sketch for SketchUp immerse you in a virtual representation of your design, providing a new perspective on the spatial dynamics of your home.

Community and Support Networks

Building a barndominium is a journey best shared. These communities and support networks can offer guidance, moral support, and a sense of camaraderie as you navigate the challenges and triumphs of your project:

- **Local Meetups and Groups**: Platforms like Meetup can help you connect with local building enthusiasts, DIYers, and professionals, offering opportunities for in-person advice and networking.
- **Online Communities**: Beyond forums, social media groups on platforms like Facebook or Instagram can connect you with a global community of barndominium builders, where members share their progress, challenges, and solutions.

Continuing Education and Workshops

The construction landscape is always evolving, with new techniques, materials, and regulations emerging. Staying informed and educated is key to a successful build. The resources below can help you stay on top of the latest developments in the field:

- **Online Courses**: Websites like Coursera and Udemy offer courses on architecture, interior design, and construction management taught by industry professionals.
- **Workshops**: Local hardware stores, community colleges, and building supply companies often host workshops and seminars on various aspects of home building, from framing to plumbing and electrical work.

In wrapping up this exploration of resources and tools, it's clear that building a barndominium is a multifaceted endeavor enriched by the wealth of knowledge, creativity, and support available to you. Whether it's through the pages of a guidebook, the interactive layout of a floor plan tool, the shared wisdom of an online forum, or the hands-on learning of a workshop, each resource plays a pivotal role in bringing your dream home to fruition. As you move forward, armed with these tools, remember that the strength of your project lies not just in the bricks and mortar but in the vision, planning, and community that underpin it.

Keeping the Game Alive

Now you have everything you need to build your dream barndominium, it's time to pass on your newfound knowledge and show other readers where they can find the same help.

Simply by leaving your honest opinion of this book on Amazon, you'll show other aspiring barndominium builders where they can find the information they're looking for, and pass their passion for creating unique homes forward.

Thank you for your help. The passion for barndominiums is thriving and grows as we share our knowledge – and you're helping us to do just that.

Scan the QR code to leave your review.

As a thank you for buying The Barndominium Builder's Handbook, we have an exclusive bonus for you. Unlock your free Barndominium Builder's Planner with this QR code.

Conclusion

Ah, what a ride it's been, folks! From the moment you cracked open the spine of this book, embarking on the roller coaster of turning barn dreams into barndominium realities, we've traversed a whole countryside of ideas together. I hope you've found that unique appeal of barndominiums as intoxicating as I do—a perfect blend of rustic barn charm and the sleek, comfy efficiencies of modern living. It's like having your cake and eating it too, but in this case, the cake is a house, and you can live in it (and honestly, isn't that just a bit better?).

Throughout our journey, we've tackled everything but the kitchen sink—and then, of course, we went ahead and tackled that, too. From deciphering the cryptic language of local regulations to pouring over the aesthetics of your future living room, we've covered the A to Z of building your dream barndo. We've chatted about the nitty-gritty of choosing the right materials (because, let's face it, not all woods are created equal) and danced through the minefield, which is the construction process.

But here's the kicker—despite the potential for gray hairs and the occasional "What in the world have I gotten myself into?" moment, building your dream barndominium is as achievable as finishing this book. Yes, it requires planning, a bit of budget wizardry, and a vision clearer than my grandma's crystal, but hey, you've got this. Remember, every big dream starts with a single, sometimes shaky, step forward.

And let's not forget about decking out your barndo in a way that screams "you." This is your chance to go green in more ways than one, with sustainability options that would make Mother Nature proud and design choices that reflect your unique taste. Your barndominium isn't just a house; it's a statement, a slice of personal paradise.

Now, I won't leave you to wander the vast plains of barndominium building alone. Dive into the community of fellow enthusiasts! There's a whole world out there brimming with support, inspiration, and tales of triumph (and the occasional misstep, which are equally valuable). The camaraderie found in these spaces is as comforting as a warm blanket on a cold night.

As for what's next, keep your mind as open as your floor plan. The world of barndominium building is ever-evolving, with new technologies, materials, and design ideas popping up like daisies. Staying informed means staying ahead and ready to tackle whatever challenge or opportunity comes your way.

So, dear reader, it's time—time to sketch, plan, and dream. Whether you're about to call up a realtor, dust off your drafting table, or simply mull over ideas with a cup of coffee in hand, you're on the precipice of something great. Your barndominium journey is just beginning, and I can't wait to see where it takes you.

From my heart to yours, remember that the process is a part of the adventure. Embrace it, with all its ups and downs, because at the end of the day, you're creating more than just a home. You're crafting a haven that's entirely, beautifully, and undeniably yours. Here's to the journey ahead, to the challenges, the triumphs, and everything in between. Cheers to you and your barndominium dream!

As you embark on your barndominium building journey, be sure to check out these two indispensable companions, also crafted by the author.

The first is a **Room Planner**, designed to help you plan every detail of each room, from layouts and purchases to tasks, quotes, and notes.

The second is a **Construction Tracker**, offering a comprehensive overview with checklists for pre-construction and construction phases, contractor details, payment tracking, and final inspections. These tools are perfect for keeping all your project details organized and ensuring a smooth building experience. Simply scan the QR codes to access these invaluable resources!

Glossary

Chiaroscuro:

- **Definition**: An artistic technique that contrasts light and dark to create a sense of volume and three-dimensionality.
- **Application**: In interior design, chiaroscuro can be used to highlight architectural features and create dramatic lighting effects, emphasizing the rustic yet modern elements of a barndominium.

Eclectic:

- **Definition**: A design style that mixes various elements from different styles and periods.
- **Application**: Combining diverse furniture, fabrics, and decor to create a unique and personalized interior in a barndominium.

Farmhouse Style:

- **Definition**: A design style that evokes the simplicity and charm of rural farmhouses.
- **Application**: Using reclaimed wood, vintage decor, and a neutral color palette to create a cozy, inviting atmosphere in a barndominium.

Green Building:

- **Definition**: A building designed to reduce the overall impact on human health and the natural environment through efficient use of energy, water, and other resources, as well as reducing waste and environmental degradation.
- **Application**: Using sustainable materials, energy-efficient systems, and eco-friendly construction practices to create an environmentally responsible barndominium.

Industrial:

- **Definition**: A design style that combines raw, unfinished elements with modern touches.
- **Application**: Using exposed beams, metal accents, and reclaimed wood to create a stylish, yet functional, industrial look in a barndominium.

Lofting:

- **Definition**: The process of creating a loft, which is a space directly under the roof of a building, often open to the floor below and used for additional living or storage space.
- **Application**: Incorporating a loft space in a barndominium for a bedroom, office, or storage area, maximizing the use of vertical space and adding a cozy, elevated area.

Low-E (Low Emissivity)

- **Definition:** Low-E refers to a type of coating applied to glass surfaces that minimizes the amount of infrared and ultraviolet light that can pass through without compromising the amount of visible light transmitted. Low-E coatings help in reflecting heat back to its source, thereby improving thermal performance and energy efficiency.
- **Importance in Barndominiums:** Incorporating Low-E glass in windows and doors of barndominiums significantly enhances energy efficiency by reducing heat transfer. This results in lower energy costs for heating and cooling, as well as improved indoor comfort. Low-E glass also helps protect furnishings from fading by blocking harmful UV rays.
- **Example:** Windows with Low-E coatings can reduce energy loss by as much as 30-50% compared to regular glass windows.

Minimalism:

- **Definition**: A design approach focused on simplicity, functionality, and the elimination of excess.
- **Application**: Using clean lines, neutral colors, and uncluttered spaces to create a serene and efficient living environment in a barndominium.

Modern Farmhouse:

- **Definition**: A contemporary take on traditional farmhouse design.
- **Application**: Combining clean lines and modern amenities with rustic materials and vintage touches to create a stylish and functional barndominium.

Open Beam:

- **Definition**: Exposed structural beams that are left visible in the interior space.
- **Application**: Highlighting the architectural elements of a barndominium and adding a rustic, industrial feel.

Open Concept:

- **Definition**: An architectural design that eliminates barriers like walls and doors to create a more expansive and fluid living space.
- **Application**: Designing large, open living areas that allow for flexible use of space and better natural light flow in a barndominium.

Passive Solar:

- **Definition**: A design approach that uses the sun's energy for the heating and cooling of living spaces by means of building orientation, window placement, and thermal mass.
- **Application**: Designing a barndominium with large south-facing windows, thermal mass walls, and proper insulation to maximize natural heating and cooling.

Patina:

- **Definition**: The surface appearance of something grown beautiful with age or use.
- **Application**: Embracing the natural aging of materials like metal and wood to add character and depth to the barndominium's interior.

Prefab (Prefabricated):

- **Definition**: Buildings or components that are manufactured off-site in advance, usually in standard sections that can be easily shipped and assembled.
- **Application**: Utilizing prefabricated components like wall panels, roof trusses, and complete modules to streamline the construction process and reduce build time for a barndominium.

Reclaimed Materials:

- **Definition**: Materials that have been salvaged from previous use and repurposed in new construction.
- **Application**: Using reclaimed wood, metal, and other materials to add character and reduce the environmental impact of building a barndominium.

R-Value:

- **Definition**: A measure of thermal resistance, indicating the effectiveness of insulation material in resisting heat flow. The higher the R-value, the better the insulation.
- **Application**: Selecting insulation materials with high R-values for walls, roofs, and floors to improve the energy efficiency of a barndominium.

Rustic Modern:

- **Definition**: A blend of rustic and contemporary design elements.
- **Application**: Combining natural materials like wood and stone with sleek, modern fixtures and open floor plans to achieve a cozy yet sophisticated look.

Shabby Chic:

- **Definition**: A design style that uses vintage furnishings and soft, muted colors to create a charming, lived-in look.
- **Application**: Incorporating distressed furniture, pastel colors, and floral patterns to add a touch of elegance and comfort to a barndominium.

Structural Insulated Panels (SIPs)

- **Definition**: Structural Insulated Panels (SIPs) are high-performance building panels used in floors, walls, and roofs for residential and light commercial buildings. Each panel consists of an insulating foam core sandwiched between two structural facings, typically oriented strand board (OSB). SIPs offer superior R-value, which measures the panel's resistance to heat flow, resulting in highly energy-efficient building envelopes.
- **Application**: SIPs are used in constructing barndominiums, stick-frame houses, and hybrid structures. They are easier to install than traditional cladding materials and provide better insulation. SIPs are screwed to framing members, and the seams are sealed with special tape to ensure airtightness. This makes them an excellent choice for builders aiming to create energy-efficient homes with tight energy envelopes. SIPs can be used in walls, roofs, and floors, providing a continuous layer of insulation and structural support.

Smart Home:

- **Definition**: A residence equipped with devices that can be controlled remotely by a smartphone, tablet, or computer, often integrating automation systems for lighting, heating, security, and appliances.
- **Application**: Incorporating smart thermostats, automated lighting, security systems, and connected appliances to enhance the functionality and efficiency of a barndominium.

Sustainable Design:

- **Definition**: An approach to design that prioritizes environmental responsibility and resource efficiency.
- **Application**: Using eco-friendly materials, energy-efficient systems, and sustainable building practices to create an environmentally conscious barndominium.

Transitional Design:

- **Definition**: A blend of traditional and contemporary styles to create a timeless look.

- **Application**: Mixing classic elements like wood paneling with modern features like sleek lighting to achieve a balanced and elegant barndominium design.

U-Value

- **Definition:** U-Value, also known as thermal transmittance, is a measure of the rate of heat transfer through a building component, such as a wall, window, roof, or door. It is expressed in watts per square meter per degree Celsius ($W/m^2 \cdot {}^\circ C$). The lower the U-Value, the better the material is at insulating and reducing heat loss.
- **Importance in Barndominiums:** In barndominium construction, selecting materials with low U-Values is crucial for improving energy efficiency. Lower U-Values help maintain a consistent indoor temperature, reduce heating and cooling costs, and enhance overall comfort.
- **Example:** A double-glazed window with a U-Value of $1.6\ W/m^2 \cdot {}^\circ C$ is more energy-efficient compared to a single-glazed window with a U-Value of $5.0\ W/m^2 \cdot {}^\circ C$.

Upcycling:

- **Definition**: The process of transforming waste materials or unwanted products into new materials or products of higher quality or environmental value.
- **Application**: Repurposing old barn wood, metal, or other materials to create unique furniture and decor items for a barndominium, adding character and reducing waste.

Wabi-Sabi:

- **Definition**: A Japanese aesthetic that finds beauty in imperfection and transience.
- **Application**: Incorporating natural materials, aged finishes, and asymmetrical designs to embrace the rustic and imperfect charm of a barndominium.

References

"10 Cutting-Edge, Energy-Efficient Building Materials." *HowStuffWorks*, 8 Feb. 2011, https://home.howstuffworks.com/home-improvement/construction/green/10-cutting-edge-building-materials.htm.

Alexander, John. "9 Questions To Ask Before Hiring A Barndominium Builder." *Green Building Elements*, 6 Sept. 2023, https://greenbuildingelements.com/questions-before-hiring-barndominium-builder/.

Alpinebuilders. "Building A Barndominium – Step By Step." *Alpine Builders*, 29 Apr. 2021, https://alpinebuilders.com/building-a-barndominium-step-by-step/.

Barndominium Kits Vs. Custom Builds: Which Is The Better Choice? https://www.simpleshowing.com/blog/barndominium-kits-vs-custom-builds-which-is-the-better-choice.

Barndominium Plans: The Best Barndominium Designs (2024). https://www.advancedhouseplans.com/collections/barndominiums.

Brand Plan Team. *How to Budget for Building a Barndominium - Barndo Plans*. 19 June 2023, https://mybarndoplans.com/how-to-budget-for-building-a-barndominium/.

Christie, Jim. *Building the Barndominium Step 1 – Preparing the Site and Getting Ready to Pour the Foundation – Mother Earth News*. https://www.motherearthnews.com/homesteading-and-livestock/building-the-barndominium-step-1-preparing-the-site-getting-ready-to-pour-the-foundation/.

"Creative Heating and Cooling Solutions for Your Barndominium Interior." *Tiny House Plans*, 10 Dec. 2023, https://www.tinyhouseplans.com/post/creative-heating-and-cooling-solutions-for-your-barndominium-interior.

Euler, Brianna. *Choosing the Right Roof for Your Barndominium*. 23 Oct. 2023, https://buildmax.com/choosing-the-right-roof-for-your-barndominium/.

Gillman, Todd. "How to Build a Barndominium: Process, Steps, Options." *Today's Homeowner*, 17 Aug. 2021, https://todayshomeowner.com/blog/guides/how-to-build-a-barndominium/.

Gordon, Alli. *9 Design Tips for Your Barndominium | SmartBuild Systems*. 3 Oct. 2023, https://smartbuildsystems.com/9-design-tips-for-the-interior-of-your-barndominium/.

"Green Principles for Residential Design | WBDG - Whole Building Design Guide." *Whole Building Design Guide*, 5 Aug. 2016, https://www.wbdg.org/resources/green-principles-residential-design.

Greenfield, Matt. "Barndominium Cost vs House: Detailed Cost Comparison Guide." *Today's Homeowner*, 10 Aug. 2021, https://todayshomeowner.com/blog/guides/barndominium-cost-vs-house/.

Hazen, Tamatha. "How Much Does a Barndominium Cost to Build? (2024)." *HomeGuide*, 13 Oct. 2023, https://homeguide.com/costs/barndominium-cost.

Homes, Alair. "Tips For Creating an Indoor-Outdoor Living Space That Boosts Your Home's Value and Your Mood." *Kirkland*, 7 June 2023, https://www.alairhomes.com/kirkland/2023/06/07/tips-for-creating-an-indoor-outdoor-living-space-that-boosts-your-homes-value-and-your-mood/.

Land Package for Barndominium - Top 14 Things to Consider. 21 May 2019, https://www.barndominiumlife.com/land-package-for-barndominium/.

"LED Lighting." *Energy.Gov*, https://www.energy.gov/energysaver/led-lighting.

Marcos, Adam. "Barndominium Foundations Guide (5 Types) BarndominiumZONE." *BarndominiumZONE.Com*, 6 Sept. 2023, https://barndominiumzone.com/foundations/.

Mitchell, Jason. "Barndominium Design Trends for 2023." *Oak n Steel*, https://www.oaknsteelbarndos.com/blog/barndominium-design-trends-for-2023.

"Navigating Barndominium Permits and Codes." *Barndominium.Design*, https://barndominium.design/permits.

O'Connor, Michael. *8 Amazing Barndominium Landscaping Ideas.* 29 Aug. 2023, https://www.barndominiumlife.com/barndominium-landscaping-ideas/.

O'Connor, Michael. *Barndominium Plumbing: Your Ultimate Guide.* 6 Apr. 2022, https://www.barndominiumlife.com/barndominium-plumbing/.

Penn Dutch Structures. "Converting A Barn Into A House? Here's What You Need To Do." *Penn Dutch Structures*, 29 Apr. 2022, https://www.penndutchstructures.com/blog/converting-a-barn-into-a-house/.

Peterson, Chris. *Barndominiums: Your Guide to a Perfect, Inexpensive Dream Home.* Cool Springs Press, 2023.

Pullega, John. *The Pet-Friendly Home Features Home Buyers Want | 2-10 Blog – 2-10 Home Buyers Warranty.* 29 Nov. 2019, https://www.2-10.com/blog/pet-friendly-home-features-buyers-want-in-their-next-house/.

Raney, Rebecca Fairley. "10 Cutting-Edge, Energy-Efficient Building Materials." *HowStuffWorks*, 8 Feb. 2011, https://home.howstuffworks.com/home-improvement/construction/green/10-cutting-edge-building-materials.htm.

Rose, Gail. *Your Ultimate Guide to Barndominium Insulation.* 6 Oct. 2020, https://www.barndominiumlife.com/barndominium-insulation/.

Sam Bird, P.E. "Let's Talk about Barndominiums." *LynnEngineering*, 4 May 2023, https://lynn-engineering.com/barndominium-framing/#:~:

Scott, Aaron. *The Interesting History of Barndominium Kits in America*. 6 Feb. 2024, https://buildmax.com/the-interesting-history-of-barndominium-kits-in-america/.

Smart Home Tips for Saving Energy | ENERGY STAR. https://www.energystar.gov/products/smart_home_tips.

Theron, Tenille. "12 Multipurpose Room Ideas for Optimal Functionality." *Decorilla Online Interior Design*, 4 Aug. 2023, https://www.decorilla.com/online-decorating/multipurpose-room-ideas-and-design/.

Trusscore. "Everything You Need to Know About Barndominiums." *Trusscore*, https://trusscore.com/blog/everything-you-need-to-know-about-barndominiums.html.

Why Effective Communication Is Vital in Construction Projects. https://www.outbuild.com/blog/why-is-communication-important-in-construction.